Contract Law

Cavendish
Publishing
Limited

First published in Great Britain 1997 by Cavendish Publishing Limited, The Glass House, Wharton Street, London WC1X 9PX.

Telephone: 0171-278 8000   Facsimile: 0171-278 8080

Lawcard on Contract law

1. Contracts – England 2. Contracts – England – Examinations, questions, etc.
I. Contract law
344.2'062

ISBN 1 85941 328 5

Printed and bound in Great Britain

Contents

1 Agreement

Offer	Acceptance

The traditional view that an agreement requires the identification of a valid offer and a valid acceptance of that offer has been challenged in recent years by:

- Lord Denning in *Gibson v Manchester City Council* (1979) and *Butler Machine Tool Co Ltd v Ex-Cell-O Corpn Ltd* (1979) where he stated that providing the parties were agreed on all material points, then there was no need for the traditional analysis.

- Lord Justice Steyn (*obiter*) in *Trentham Ltd v Archital Luxfer* (1993) where he stated that a strict analysis of offer and acceptance was not necessary in an executed contract in a commercial setting.

The traditional view, however, was applied by the House of Lords in *Gibson v Manchester City Council* (1979).

Lord Diplock did recognise that there may be some 'exceptional contracts which do not fit easily into an analysis of offer and acceptance', eg a multipartite contract as in *Clarke v Dunraven* (1897), but he stressed that in most contracts the 'conventional' approach of seeking an offer and an acceptance of that offer must be adhered to.

> In normal cases, therefore, a valid offer and a valid acceptance of that offer must be identified.

Unilateral and bilateral agreements

A bilateral agreement consists of an exchange of promises, eg	**In a unilateral agreement** the offeror alone makes a promise. The offer is accepted by doing what is set out in the offer, eg
Offer – I will sell my car for £500.	Offer – I will pay £500 to anyone who returns my lost kitten.
Acceptance – I will give you £500 for your car.	Acceptance – The lost kitten is returned.

The distinction is important with regard to:

- advertisements;
- revocation of offers;
- communication of acceptance.

Offer

> A definite promise to be bound by provided that certain specified terms are accepted.

A valid offer:

- Must be communicated, so that the offeree may accept or reject it.
- May be communicated in writing, orally, or by conduct.

There is no general requirement that an agreement must be in writing.

- May be made to a particular person, to a group of persons, or to the whole world. In *Carlill v Carbolic Smoke Ball Co Ltd* (1893) the defendants issued an advertisement in which they offered to pay £100 to any person who used their smoke balls and then succumbed to influenza. Mrs Carlill, who had seen the advertisement and used the smoke ball, had immediately gone down with influenza. She sued for the £100. The defendants argued that it was not possible in English law to make an offer to the whole world. Held – an offer can be made to the whole world.

- Must be definite in substance (see certainty of terms, below).

- Must be distinguished from an invitation to treat.

Invitations to treat

> An indication that the invitor is willing to enter into negotiations but is not prepared to be bound.

In *Gibson v Manchester City Council* (1979) the council's letter stated 'we may be prepared to sell you ...'.

A response to an invitation to treat does not lead to an agreement. The response itself may be an offer.

The distinction between an offer and an invitation to treat depends on the intention of the parties. This must be judged objectively.

The courts have already established that there is no intention to be bound in the following cases.

Display of goods for sale
- In a shop. In *Pharmaceutical Society of GB v Boots Cash Chemists Ltd* (1952) the Court of Appeal held that in a self-service shop, the sale takes place when the assistant accepts the customer's offer to buy the goods. The goods on the shelves are mere invitations to treat.

- In a shop window. In *Fisher v Bell* (1961) it was held that a 'flick knife' displayed in a shop window with a price attached was an invitation to treat.

However, it was suggested by Lord Denning in *Thornton v Shoe Lane Parking* (1971) (see below) that vending machines and automatic ticket machines are offers since once the money has been inserted the transaction is irrevocable.

- In an advertisement. In *Partridge v Crittenden* (1968) an advertisement which said 'Bramblefinche cocks and hens – 25s' was held to be an invitation to treat. The court pointed out that if the advertisement was treated as an offer this could lead to many actions for breach of contract against the advertiser, as his stock of birds was limited; so he could not have intended the advertisement to be an offer.

However, if the advertisement is unilateral in nature, then the advertisement will be an offer. See *Carlill v Carbolic Smoke Ball Co Ltd* (above). Advertising a reward may also be a unilateral offer.

Auctions

- An auctioneer's request for bids in *Payne v Cave* (1789) was held to be an invitation to treat. The offer was made by the bidder.

- A notice of an auction. In *Harris v Nickerson* (1873) it was held that a notice that an auction would be held on a certain date was not an offer which then could be accepted by turning up at the stated time. It was a statement of intention.

However, if the auction is stated to be 'without reserve' then there is still no necessity to hold an auction, but if the auction is held, it must be 'without reserve' (*Warlow v Harrison* (1859)). The phrase 'without reserve' has been interpreted as a unilateral offer which can be accepted by turning up and submitting the highest bid.

Tenders

A request for tenders is normally an invitation to treat.

- However, it was held in *Harvela Ltd v Royal Trust of Canada* (1985) that if the request is made to specified parties and it is stated that the contract will be awarded to the lowest or the highest bidder, then this will be binding as an implied unilateral offer. It was also held in that case that a referential bid eg 'the highest other bid plus 10%' was not a valid bid.

- It was also held in *Blackpool and Fylde Aero Club v Blackpool BC* (1990) that if the request is addressed to specified parties, this amounts to a unilateral offer that serious consideration will be given to each tender.

Subject to contract
- The words 'subject to contract' may be placed on top of a letter in order to indicate that certain offers are not to be to be legally binding (*Walford v Miles* (1992)).

Termination of the offer

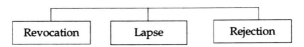

Revocation (termination by the offeror)
An offeror may withdraw an offer at any time before it has been accepted.

- The revocation must be communicated to the offeree before acceptance. In *Byrne v van Tienhoven* (1880) the withdrawal of an offer sent by telegram was held to be communicated only when the telegram was received.

- Communication need not be made by the offeror; communication through a third party will suffice. In *Dickinson v Dodds* (1876) the plaintiff was told by a neighbour that a farm which had been offered to him had been sold to a third party. Held – the offer had been validly revoked.

- An offer to keep an offer open for a certain length of time can be withdrawn like any other unless an option has been purchased, eg consideration has been given to keep the offer open.

Unilateral offers
- Communication of the revocation is difficult if the offer was to the whole world. It was suggested, however, in the American case of *Shuey v USA* (1875) that communication will be assumed if the offeror takes reasonable

steps to inform the public, eg places an advertisement in the same newspaper.

- It now seems established that revocation cannot take place if the offeree has started to perform. In *Errington v Errington* (1952) a father promised his daughter and son-in-law that if they paid off the mortgage on a house he owned, he would give it to them. The young couple duly paid the instalments, but the offer was withdrawn shortly before the whole debt was paid. Held – there was an implied term in the offer that it was irrevocable once performance had begun. This is also supported by *dicta* in *Daulia v Four Milbank Nominees* (1978).

Lapse (termination by operation of law)

An offer may lapse and thus be incapable of being accepted because of:

- Passage of time
  - ○ at the end of a stipulated time (if any); or
  - ○ if no time is stipulated, after a reasonable time. In *Ramsgate Victoria Hotel Co v Montefiore* (1866) an attempt to accept an offer to buy shares after five months failed as the offer had clearly lapsed.

- Death
  - ○ of the offeror if the offer was of a personal nature;
  - ○ of the offeree.

- Failure of a condition
  - ○ an express condition; or
  - ○ an implied condition. In *Financings Ltd v Stimson* (1962) it was held that an offer to buy a car lapsed

when the car was badly damaged on the ground that the offer contained an implied term that the car would remain in the same condition as when the offer was made.

Rejection (termination by the offeree)
A rejection may be:

- express;

- implied.

A counter offer is an implied rejection
- Traditionally an acceptance must be a mirror image of the offer. If any alteration is made or anything added, then this will be a counter offer, and will terminate the offer. In *Hyde v Wrench* (1840) the defendant offered to sell a farm for £1,000. The plaintiff said he would give £950 for it. Held – this was a counter offer which terminated the original offer which was therefore no longer open for acceptance. In *Brogden v Metropolitan Railway* (1877) the defendant sent to the plaintiff for signature a written agreement which they had negotiated. The plaintiff signed the agreement and entered in the name of an arbitrator on a space which had been left empty for this purpose. Held – the returned document was not an acceptance but a counter offer.

- This is particularly important for businesses who contract by means of sales forms and purchase forms, eg if an order placed by the buyer's purchase form is 'accepted' on the seller's sales form, and the conditions on the back of the two forms are not identical (which they are very unlikely to be) then the 'acceptance' is a counter offer ie an implied rejection. In *Butler Machine Tool Co Ltd v Ex-Cell-O Corpn Ltd* (1979) the sellers offered to sell a machine tool to the buyers for £75,535 on their own conditions of sale which were stated to prevail over any conditions in the buyers' order form, and which contained a price variation clause. The buyers 'accepted' their offer on their own order form which stated that the price was a fixed price, and which contained a tear off slip which said 'we accept your order on the terms and conditions stated thereon'. The sellers signed and returned the slip together with a letter which stated that they were carrying out the order in accordance with their original offer. When they delivered the machine they claimed the price had increased by £2,892. The buyers refused to pay the extra sum. Held – the contract was concluded on the buyers' terms; the signing and returning of the tear-off slip was conclusive. The court analysed the transaction by applying the 'mirror image' rules.

Note – a request for further information is not a counter offer. In *Stevenson v McLean* (1880) the defendant offered to sell to the plaintiff iron at 40s a ton. The plaintiff telegraphed to enquire whether he could pay by instalments. Held – this was a mere enquiry for information, not a counter offer.

A conditional or qualified acceptance
A conditional acceptance may be a counter offer capable of acceptance, eg I will pay £500 for your car if you paint it red; or it may be a qualified acceptance as in the phrase 'subject to contract'.

Acceptance

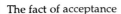

| The fact of acceptance | Communication of acceptance |

The fact of acceptance

> An acceptance is a final and unqualified assent to all
> the terms of the offer.

A valid acceptance must:

- be made while the offer is still in force
  (see termination of offer, above);

- be made by the offeree;

- exactly match the terms of the offer, eg it must be a 'mirror image' of the offer (see counter offers, above);

- be written, oral, or implied from conduct. In *Brogden v Metropolitan Railway* (1877) (above) the returned document was held to be a counter offer which the defendants then accepted either by ordering coal from Brogden or by accepting delivery of the coal (see also 'The Battle of the Forms').

However, the offeror may require the acceptance to be made in a certain way. If the requirement is mandatory, it must be followed.

If the requirement is directory, then another equally effective method will suffice. In *Manchester Diocesan Council for Education v Commercial and General Investments Ltd* (1969) an invitation to tender stated that the person whose bid was accepted would be informed by a letter to the address given in the tender. The acceptance was eventually sent not to this address but to the defendant's surveyor. Held – the statement in the tender was not mandatory; the tender had therefore been validly accepted.

- Where the offer is made in alternative terms, the acceptance must make it clear to which set of terms it relates.

- A person cannot accept an offer of which he has no knowledge (*Clarke* (1927) (Australia)).

But a person's motive in accepting the offer is irrelevant. In *Williams v Carwardine* (1833) (Australia) the plaintiff knew of the offer of a reward in exchange for information, but her motive was to salve her conscience. Held – she was entitled to the reward.

- 'Cross-offers' do not constitute an agreement (*Tinn v Hoffman & Co* (1873)).

Communication of acceptance

> Acceptance must be communicated.

Acceptance must be communicated by the offeree or his agent. In *Powell v Lee* (1908) an unauthorised communication by one of the managers that the Board of Managers had selected a particular candidate for a head ship was held not to be a valid acceptance.

Silence as communication

An offeror may not stipulate that silence of the offeree is to amount to acceptance. In *Felthouse v Bindley* (1862) the plaintiff wrote to his nephew offering to buy a horse, and adding, 'If I hear no more ... I will take it that the horse is mine.' The nephew did not reply to this letter. Held – no contract. Acceptance had not been communicated to the offeror.

It has been suggested that this does not mean that silence can never amount to acceptance, eg if in *Felthouse v Bindley* the offeree had relied on the offeror's statement that he need not communicate his acceptance, and wished to claim acceptance on that basis, the court could interpret that the need for acceptance had been waived by the offeror (see below).

Exceptions to the rule that acceptance must be communicated

- Where communication is expressly (see above *Felthouse v Bindley*) or impliedly (see *Carlill v Carbolic Smoke Ball Co* above) waived.

- Where failure of communication is the fault of the offeror. This was suggested by Lord Denning in *Entores Ltd v Miles Far East Corpn* (1955).

- Where the post is deemed to be the proper method of communication. In *Adams v Lindsell* (1818) the defendants wrote to the plaintiffs offering to sell them a quantity of wool and requiring acceptance by post. The plaintiffs immediately posted an acceptance on 5 December. Held – the contract was completed on 5 December.

The postal rule

> Acceptance takes place when a letter is posted, not when it is received.

- *Adams v Lindsell* (1818), above.

- Acceptance is effective on posting, even when the letter is lost in the post. In *Household Fire Insurance Co Ltd v Grant* (1879) the defendant offered to buy shares in the plaintiff's company. A letter of allotment was posted to the defendant, but it never reached him. Held – the contract was completed when the letter was posted.

- Note the interplay between acceptance and revocation by post:
  - ○ Acceptance takes place when a letter is posted.
  - ○ Revocation takes place when the letter is received.

Byrne v van Tienhoven (1880), above.

Limitations to the postal rule
- It only applies to letters and telegrams. It does not apply to instantaneous methods of communication).

- It must be reasonable to use the post as the means of communication (eg an offer by telephone or by fax might indicate that a rapid method of response was required).

- Letters of acceptance must be properly addressed and stamped.

- The rule is easily displaced, eg it may be excluded by the offeror either expressly or impliedly. In *Holwell Securities Ltd v Hughes* (1974) it was excluded by the offeror requiring 'notice in writing'. It was also suggested by the court that the rule would not be used where it would lead to manifest inconvenience.

> Query – can a letter of acceptance be cancelled by actual communication before the letter is delivered?

There is no direct English authority on this point.

Logic – once a letter is posted the offer is accepted; there is no provision in law for revoking an acceptance.

- It was not accepted in the New Zealand case of *Wenckheim v Arndt* (1878) nor in the South African case of *A to Z Bazaars (Pty) Ltd v Minister of Agriculture* (1974).

- Chesire argues that it would be unfair to the offeror, who would be bound as soon as the letter was posted, but would allow the offeree to keep his options open.

Arguments for

It was allowed in the Scottish case of *Countess of Dunmore v Alexander* (1830).

- It is argued that actual prior communication of rejection would not necessarily prejudice the offeror. Treitel sees no reason why a rule setting out the relationship between revocation and acceptance and what happens when a letter is lost in the post should also govern cancellation of an acceptance by post.

- It is also argued that it would be absurd to insist on enforcing a contract when both parties had acted on the recall. This, however, could be interpreted as an agreement to discharge.

Communication by instantaneous/electronic means

Acceptance takes place when and where the message is received.

- The rules on telephones and telex were laid down in *Entores v Miles* (above) and confirmed in *Brinkibon Ltd v*

Stahag Stahl (1983) where it was held that during normal office hours, acceptance takes place when the message is printed out not when it is read. The House of Lords, however, accepted that communication by telex may not always be instantaneous, eg when received at night or when the office is closed.

- Lord Wilberforce stated:

  'No universal rule could cover all such cases; they must be resolved by reference to the intention of the parties, by sound business practice, and in some cases, by a judgment of where the risk should lie.'

- It has been suggested that a message sent outside business hours should be 'communicated' when it is expected that it would be read, eg at the next opening of business. It is generally accepted that the same rules should relate to faxes as to telex.

- There is no direct authority on telephone answering machines. On one hand it is argued that the presence of an answering machine indicates that communication is not instantaneous; there is a delay between sending and receiving messages. It has been suggested that until the matter is dealt with by the court, the basic rule should apply, ie that acceptance must be communicated. Acceptance, therefore, takes place when the message is actually heard by the offeror.

Certainty of terms

It is for the parties to make their intentions clear.

The courts will not enforce:

Vague agreements eg	Incomplete agreements eg
Scammell v Ouston (1941) The courts refused to enforce a sale stated to be made 'on hire purchase terms'; neither the rate of interest, not the period of repayment, nor the number of instalments were stated.	'an agreement to make an agreement' will be void. In *Walford v Miles* (1992) the court refused to enforce an 'agreement to negotiate in good faith'. See also *May and Butcher v R* (1934).

But the uncertainty may be cured by:

- a trade custom, where a word has a specific meaning.

- previous dealings between the parties whereby a word or phrase has acquired a specific meaning, eg timber of 'fair specification' in *Hillas v Arcos* (1932).

- the contract itself, which provides a method for resolving an uncertainty. In *Foley v Classique Coaches* (1934) there was an executed contract where the vagueness of 'at a price to be agreed' was cured by a provision in the contract referring disputes to arbitration. *Cf May and Butcher v R*, an unexecuted contract, where the court refused to allow a similar arbitration clause to cure the uncertainty.

The courts will strive to find a contract valid where it has been executed.

- The Sale of Goods Act 1979 provides that if no price or mechanism for fixing the price is provided, then the buyer must pay a 'reasonable price', but this provision will not apply where the contract states that the price is 'to be agreed between the parties'.

- Note, a 'lock-out agreement', eg an agreement not to negotiate with any one else, is valid provided it is clearly stated and for a specific length of time. This was applied by the Court of Appeal in *Pitt v PHH Asset Management* (1993) where a promise not to negotiate with any third party for two weeks was enforced.

2 Consideration and intention

Consideration

Most legal systems will only enforce promises where there is something to indicate that the promisor intended to be bound, ie there is some:

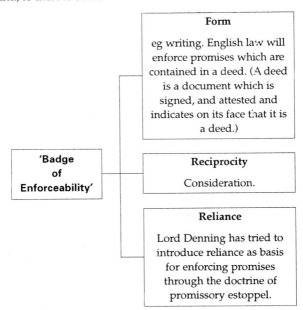

'Badge of Enforceability'

Form

eg writing. English law will enforce promises which are contained in a deed. (A deed is a document which is signed, and attested and indicates on its face that it is a deed.)

Reciprocity

Consideration.

Reliance

Lord Denning has tried to introduce reliance as basis for enforcing promises through the doctrine of promissory estoppel.

Consideration is the normal 'Badge of Enforceability' in English law.

Definitions of consideration

> A valuable consideration in the eyes of the law may consist of:
>
> either some right, interest, profit or benefit to one party; or
>
> some forbearance, detriment, loss or responsibility given, suffered or undertaken by the other.

Shorter version:

> A benefit to one party or a detriment to the other.

Limitation of the definition

- It makes no mention of why the promisee incurs a detriment or confers a benefit, or that the element of a bargain is central to the classical notion of consideration, eg in *Combe v Combe* (1951) it was held that there was no consideration for the defendant's promise to pay his ex-wife £100 per year even though in reliance on that promise she had not applied to the divorce court for maintenance, and in that sense she had suffered a detriment. The reason why the detriment did not constitute consideration was that there was no request by the husband, express or implied, that she should forbear from applying for maintenance. There was no 'exchange'.

- Some writers have preferred to emphasise this element of bargain and have defined consideration as the

> 'the element of exchange in a contract'
>
> or
>
> 'the price paid for a promise'

- These definitions, however, are vague, and despite its limitation the benefit/detriment definition is most commonly used.

Consideration and condition

Consideration must be distinguished from the fulfilment of a condition. If A says to B, 'I will give you £500 if you break a leg', there is no contract but simply a gratuitous promise subject to a condition. In *Carlill v Carbolic Smoke Ball Co* (1893), the plaintiff provided consideration for the defendant's promise by using the smoke-ball. Catching influenza was only a condition of her entitlement to enforce the promise.

Kinds of consideration

Executory consideration	**Executed consideration**
A promise to do something in the future.	An act wholly performed at the time the contract is entered into.

Past consideration ie something already completed before the promise is made cannot amount to consideration.

- In *Roscorla v Thomas* (1842), the defendant promised the plaintiff that a horse which had been bought by him was sound and free from vice. It was held that since this promise was made after the sale had been completed, there was not consideration for it and it could not be enforced. In *Re McArdle* (1951), a promise made 'in consideration of your carrying our certain improvements to the property' was held by the Court of Appeal to be unenforceable as all the work had been done before the promise was made.

Exception to this rule:

- In *Lampleigh v Braithwait* (1615) it was held that where a service was rendered at the request of the promisor, on the understanding that a payment would be made, a subsequent promise to pay a certain sum will be enforced on the basis that it merely fixes the amount of the payment.

- The modern requirements were laid down by Lord Scarman in *Pao On v Lau Yiu Long* (1980) where a service is rendered:

  ○ at the request of the promisor;

  ○ on the understanding that a payment will be made, and if the payment would have been legally enforceable if it had been promised in advance, then a subsequent promise to pay a certain sum will be enforced.

Note, the 'inferred' intention to pay makes this a very flexible exception.

Consideration must move from the promisee

> Only a person who has provided consideration
> for a promise can enforce that promise.

- See Chapter 10 – Privity of Contract.

Consideration need not be adequate

> The consideration provided by
> one party need not equal in value the
> consideration provided by the other party.

It is for the parties themselves to make their own bargain.
The consideration need only have 'some value in the eyes of
the law'. See 'sufficiency of consideration'.

- The value may be slight. In *Chappell Co Ltd v Nestlé Co Ltd*
  (1960) three wrappers from the defendant's chocolate
  bars were held to be part of the consideration. In
  Mountford v Scott (1975) £1 was held to be good consideration for an option to buy a house.

- Withdrawal of threatened legal proceedings will amount
  to consideration, even if the claim is found to have no
  legal basis, provided that the parties themselves believe
  that the claim is valid (*Callisher v Bischoffstein* (1870)).

- In *Pitt v PHH Asset Management* (1993) the defendant
  agreed to a lock-out agreement in return for Pitt drop-
  ping his claim for an injunction against them. The claim
  for an injunction had no merit, but had a nuisance value,
  and therefore was good consideration.

- In *Alliance Bank v Broome* (1964) the bank's forbearance to
  sue was held to be consideration for the defendant's
  promise to provide security for a loan.

There is no consideration, however, where the promises are
vague, eg 'to stop being a nuisance to his father' (*White v
Bluett* (1853) but cf *Ward v Byham* (1956) below) or illusory, eg

to do something impossible, or merely good, eg to show love or affection or gratitude.

It has been argued that because the latter are invalid, that consideration must have some economic value. But economic value is extremely difficult to discern in the other cases cited above. Since consideration is a 'badge of enforceability', it is argued that nominal consideration is adequate; it is only designed to show that the promise is intended to be legally enforceable; whether it creates any economic advantage is therefore irrelevant.

> Consideration, therefore, is found
> when a person receives whatever he requests
> in return for a promise whether or not it has an
> economic value, provided it is not too vague.

Consideration must be sufficient

> The consideration must have
> some value in the eyes of the law.

Traditionally the following have no value in the eyes of the law:

Performing a duty imposed by law	Performing an existing contractual duty

Performing a duty imposed by law

- eg promising not to commit a crime, or promising to appear in court after being subpoenaed. In *Collins v Godefroy* (1831), a promise to pay a fee to a witness who has been properly subpoenaed to attend a trial was held to have been made without consideration. The witness had a public duty to attend.

- But if a person does, or promises to do, more than he is required to do by law, then he is providing consideration. In *Glasbrook Bros v Glamorgan CC* (1925), the council, as police authority, on the insistence of a colliery owner, and in return for a promise of payment, provided protection over and above that required by law. Held – they had provided consideration for the promise to pay.

- In *Ward v Byham* (1956), the father of an illegitimate child promised to pay the mother an allowance of £1 per week if she proved that the child was 'well-looked after and happy'. Held – the mother was entitled to enforce the promise because in undertaking to see that the child was 'well-looked after and happy', she was doing more than her legal obligation. Lord Denning, however, based his decision on the ground that the mother provided consideration by performing her legal duty to maintain the child.

Treitel agrees with Denning that performance of a duty imposed by the law can be consideration for a promise. He argues that it is public policy which accounts for the refusal of the law in certain circumstances to enforce promises to perform existing duties. Where there are no grounds of public policy involved, then a promise given in consideration of a public duty can be enforced.

He cites:

- promises to pay rewards for information leading to the arrest of a felon. See *Sykes v DPP* (1961);

- *Ward v Byham* (above).

In most cases, it would make no difference whether the court proceeded on the basis that the matter was one of public policy or a lack of consideration. But the former ground does allow a greater degree of flexibility.

Performing an existing contractual duty

This cannot be consideration for:

A request for extra payment	A request to avoid part of debt

A request for extra payment
- In *Stilk v Myrick* (1809), the captain promised the rest of crew extra wages if they would sail the ship back home. after two sailors had deserted. Held – the crew were already bound by their contract to meet the normal emergencies of the voyage and were doing no more than their original contractual duty in working the ship home.

- Where the promisor, however, performs more than he had originally promised, then there can be consideration. In *Hartley v Ponsonby* (1857), nearly half the crew deserted. This discharged the contracts of the remaining sailors as it was dangerous to sail the ship home with only half the crew. The sailors were therefore free to make a new bargain, so the captain's promise to pay them additional wages was enforceable.

Exceptions to the rule in *Stilk v Meyrick*:

Factual advantages obtained by the promisor
In *Williams v Roffey Bros* (1991), the defendants (the main contractors) were refurbishing a block of flats. They sub-contracted the carpentry work to the plaintiff. The plaintiff ran

into financial difficulties, whereupon the defendants agreed to pay the plaintiff an additional sum if they completed the work on time. Held – where a party to an existing contract later agrees to pay an 'extra bonus' in order that the other party performs his obligations under the original contract, then the new agreement is binding if the party agreeing to pay the bonus has thereby obtained some new practical advantage or avoided a disadvantage. In this particular case, the advantage was the avoidance of a penalty clause and the expense of finding new carpenters.

- Note – *Stilk v Myrick* (above) recognises as consideration only those acts which the promisee was not under a legal obligation to perform. *Williams v Roffey Bros* (above) adds to these factual advantages obtained by the promisor.

- This decision pushes to the fore the principles of economic duress as a means of distinguishing extorted and non-extorted modifications to a contract (see Chapter 5 on Economic Duress).

Duties owed to third party
Where a duty is owed to a third party, its performance can also be consideration for a promise by another. It is clear that the third party is getting something more than he is entitled to.

- In *Shadwell v Shadwell* (1860), an uncle promised to pay an annual sum to his nephew on hearing of his intended marriage. The fact of the marriage provided consideration, although the nephew was already legally contracted to marry his fiance.

- In *Scotson v Pegg* (1861), A agreed to deliver coal to B's order. B ordered A to deliver coal to C who promised A to unload it. Held – A could enforce C's promise as A's delivery of the coal was good consideration, notwithstanding that he was already bound to do so by his contract with B.

- In *New Zealand Shipping Co v Satterthwaite & Co Ltd, The Euremydon* (1975), it was held by the Privy Council that where a stevedore, at the request of the shipper of the goods, removed the goods from a ship, this is consideration for the promise by the shipper not to sue him for damages, although the stevedore in removing the goods is only performing contractual duties he owes to the ship.

A request to avoid part of a debt

> Basic rule: Payment of a smaller sum
> will not discharge the duty to pay a higher sum.

If a creditor is owed £100 and agrees to accept £90 in full settlement, he can later insist on the remaining £10 being paid as there is no consideration for his promise to waive the £10 (the rule in *Pinnel's* case (1602)).

- This rule was confirmed by the House of Lords in *Foakes v Beer* (1884). Dr Foakes was indebted to Mrs Beer on a judgment sum of £2,090. It was agreed by Mrs Beer that if Foakes paid her £500 in cash and the balance of £1,590 in instalments, she would not take 'any proceedings whatsoever' on the judgment. Foakes paid the money exactly as requested, but Mrs Beer then proceeded to claim an additional £360 as interest on the judgment debt. Foakes refused and when sued, pleaded that his duty to pay interest had been discharged by the promise not to sue. Their Lordships deferred as to whether, on its true construction, the agreement merely gave Foakes time to pay or was intended to cover interest as well. But they held, even on the latter construction, there was no consideration for the promise and that Foakes was still bound to pay the additional sum.

There are situations, however, where payment of a smaller sum will discharge the liability for the higher sum:

- where the promise to accept a smaller sum in full settlement is made by deed, or in return for consideration;

- where the original claim was unliquidated or disputed in good faith;

- where the debtor does something different, eg where payment is made, at the creditor's request,

  ○ at an earlier time

  ○ at a different place

  ○ by a different method (it was held in *DC Builders Ltd v Rees* (1966) that payment by cheque is not payment by a different method);

- where payment is accompanied by a benefit of some kind;

- in a composition agreement with creditors;

- where payment is made by a third party (see *Hirachand Punamchand v Temple* (1911));

It has been argued that to allow the creditor to sue for the remaining debt would be a fraud on the third parties in the above two cases.

Note – the doctrine of promissory estoppel, under certain circumstances, may allow payment of smaller sum to discharge liability for the larger sum.

In *Re Selectmove* (1995) the Court of Appeal refused to extend the principle laid down in *Williams v Roffey Bros* to part payment of a debt. The company had offered to pay its arrears by instalments to the Inland Revenue who said that they would let them know if this was acceptable. They heard nothing further, but paid some instalments and then received a threat of being wound up if the full arrears were not paid immediately. The court was not prepared to allow *Williams v Roffey Bros* to overturn a rule laid down by the House of Lords in *Foakes v Beer*.

Promissory estoppel

> If a promise, intended to be be binding, is acted upon, then the court will not allow the promisor to go back on his promise.

There are problems with regard to:

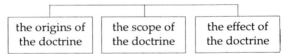

| the origins of the doctrine | the scope of the doctrine | the effect of the doctrine |

Origins

- It was introduced (*obiter*) by Lord Denning in the *Central London Property Trust Ltd v High Trees House Ltd* (1947) where owners of a block of flats had promised to accept reduced rents in 1939. There was no consideration for their promise, but Lord Denning nevertheless stated that he would estopp them from recovering any arrears. He based his statement on the decision in *Hughes v Metropolitan Railway* (1877).

- It would, however, seem to conflict with the House of Lords decision in *Jorden v Money* (1854) where it was stated that estoppel applied only to statements of fact and not to promises, and also with the decision in *Foakes v Beer* (1884) where the House of Lords confirmed that payment of a smaller sum will not discharge the liability for a larger sum.

Scope

> The exact scope of the doctrine is a matter of debate; but certain requirements must be met.

- It only applies to the modification or discharge of an existing contractual obligation. It cannot create a new contract. See *Combe v Combe* (1951) above. (However, it was used to create a new right of action in the Australian case of *Waltons v Maher* (1988).)

- It can be used as a 'shield and not a sword'.

- The promise not to enforce rights must be clear and unequivocal. In *The Scaptrade* (1983) the mere fact of not having enforced one's full rights in the past was not sufficient.

- It must be inequitable for the promisor to go back on his promise. In *D&C Builders v Rees* (1966) Mrs Rees had forced the builders to accept her cheque by inequitable means.

- The promisee must have acted in reliance on the promise, although not necessarily to his detriment (*Alan & Co Ltd v El-Nasr Export & Import Co* (1972)).

Effect of the doctrine

> It is not clear whether the doctrine extinguishes rights, or merely suspends them.

- In *Tool Metal Manufacturing Co v Tungsten Electric Co* (1955) the owner of a patent promised to suspend periodic payments during the war. It was held by the Court of Appeal that the promise was binding for the duration of the war but the owners could, on giving reasonable notice at he end of the war, revert to their original legal entitlements.

- In *Ajayi v Briscoe* (1964) the Privy Council stated that the promisee could resile from his promise on giving reasonable notice which allowed the promisee a reasonable opportunity of resuming his position, but that the promise would become final if the promisee could not resume his former position.

On one interpretation, these cases show that as regards existing or past obligations it is extinctive; but as regards future obligations it is suspensory.

On another interpretation, the correct approach is to look at the nature of the promise. If it was intended to be permanent, then the promisee's liability will be extinguished.

Lord Denning has consistently asserted that promissory estoppel can extinguish debts. However, this view is contrary to *Foakes v Beer.*

The view that promissory estoppel is suspensory only would reconcile it with the decisions in *Jorden v Money; Foakes v Beer* and *Pinnel's* case but it would deprive it of most of its usefulness.

The question of whether the doctrine is suspensory or extinctive is particularly important with regard to single payments.

Intention to be legally bound

Commercial and Business Agreements	Social and Domestic Agreements

In Commercial and Business Agreements there is a presumption that the parties intend to create legal relations.

This presumption may be rebutted but the onus of proof is on the party seeking to exclude legal relations. In *Esso Petroleum Co Ltd v Commissioners of Customs and Excise* (1976) Esso promised to give one world cup coin with every four gallons of petrol sold. A majority of the House of Lords believed that the presumption in favour of legal relations had not been rebutted.

Examples of rebuttals

- 'Agreement need not be subject to the jurisdiction of any court' (*Rose and Frank v Crompton Bros* (1925)).

- Agreement to be binding 'in honour only' (*Jones v Vernon Pools* (1939)).

- Letters of comfort, eg statements to encourage lending to an associated company. It was held in *Kleinwort Benson Ltd v Malaysia Mining Corpn* (1989) that the defendant's statement that 'it is our policy to ensure that the business is at all times in a position to meet its liabilities to you' was a statement of present fact and not a promise for the future. It was not intended to create legal relations.

- Collective agreements are declared not to be legally binding by Trade Unions and Labour Relations Act 1974.

> In social and domestic agreements there is a
> presumption against legal relations.

This can be rebutted by evidence to the contrary, eg:

- Agreements between husband and wife. In *Balfour v Balfour* (1919) the court refused to enforce a promise by the husband to give his wife £50 per month whilst he was working abroad. However, the court will enforce a clear agreement where the parties are separating or separated (*Merritt v Merritt* (1970)).

- Agreements between members of a family. In *Jones v Padavatton* (1969) Mrs Jones offered a monthly allowance to her daughter if she would come to England to read for the Bar. Her daughter agreed but was not very successful. Mrs Jones stopped paying the monthly allowance but allowed her daughter to live in her house and receive the rents from other tenants. Mrs Jones later sued for possession. The daughter counter claimed for breach of the agreement to pay the monthly allowance and/or for accommodation. Held (a) the first agreement may have been made with the intention of creating legal relations, but was for a reasonable time and would in any case have lapsed. (b) the second agreement was a family arrangement without an intention to create legal relations. It was very vague and uncertain.

- An intention to be legally bound may be inferred where one party has acted to his detriment on the agreement (*Parker v Clark* (1960)); or

  - a business arrangement is involved (*Snelling v Snelling* (1973)); or

  - there is mutuality (*Simpkins v Pays* (1955)).

But in all such cases, the agreement must be clear.

3 Contents of a contract

Once a contract has been formed. it is necessary to explore the scope of the obligations which each party incurs.

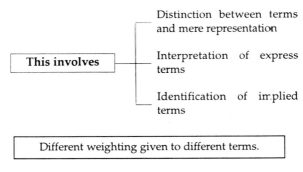

| This involves | Distinction between terms and mere representation |
| Interpretation of express terms |
| Identification of implied terms |

Different weighting given to different terms.

(Incorporation of terms is covered in Chapter 4.)

The distinction between terms and mere representations
Is the statement or assurance part of the contract? Statements made during negotiations leading to a contract may be either:

- Terms

   ie, statements which form the express terms of the contract. If these are untrue, the untruth constitutes a breach of contract; or

- Mere representations

   ie, statements which do not form part of the contract, but which helped to induce the contract. If these are untrue, they are 'misrepresentations'.

Now that damages can be awarded for negligent misrepresentation, the distinction has lost much of its former significance, but there are still some important consequences.

> Whether a statement has become a term of the contract, depends on the intention of the parties.

In trying to ascertain such intention, the court may take into account the following factors.

The importance of the statement to the parties
- In *Bannerman v White* (1861) the buyer stated 'if sulphur has been used, I do not want to know the price'. Held – a term. Similarly, in *Couchman v Hill* (1947) the buyer asked if the cow was in calf, stating that if she was, he would not bid. The auctioneer's reply that she was not in calf was held to be a term overriding the printed conditions which stated that no warranty was given (*Routledge v McKay* (1954)).

The respective knowledge of the parties
- In *Oscar Chess Ltd v Williams* (1957) it was held that a statement by a member of the public (a non expert) to a garage (an expert) with regard to the age of a car was a mere representation not a term. On the other hand, a statement made by a garage (an expert) to a member of the public (a non expert) concerning the mileage of a car was held to be a term (*Dick Bentley Productions Ltd v Harold Smith (Motors) Ltd* (1965)).

The manner of the statement
- For example – if it suggests verification (*Ecay v Godfrey* (1947)) it is unlikely to be a term. If it discourages verification, 'If there was anything wrong with the horse,

I would tell you' (*Schawel v Reade* (1913)) it is unlikely to be a term.

Where a contract has been reduced to writing

The terms will normally be the statements incorporated into the written contract (*Routledge v McKay* (1954)).

- But a contract may be partly oral and partly written (see *Couchman v Hill* (1947) above). In *Evans & Sons Ltd v Andrea Merzario Ltd* (1976) an oral assurance that machinery would be stowed under, not on the deck was held to be a term of a contract, although it was not incorporated into the written terms. The court held that the contract was partly oral and partly written, and in such hybrid circumstances the court was entitled to look at all the circumstances.

- Note, the discovery of a collateral contract may overcome the difficulties of oral warranties in written contracts. In *City of Westminster Properties v Mudd* (1959) a tenant signed a lease containing a covenant to use the premises for business premises only. He was induced to sign by a statement that this clause did not apply to him and that he could continue to sleep on the premises. The court found that his signing the contract was consideration for this promise, thus creating a collateral contract. In *Evans & Son Ltd v Andrea Merzario Ltd* (1976) Lord Denning considered the oral statement to be a collateral contract. In *Esso Petroleum Co v Mardon* (1976) the court held that the statement by a representative of Esso with regard to the throughput of a petrol station was covered by an implied collateral warranty that the statement had been made with due care and skill.

Note, acceptance by the court of a collateral contract is rare. It was stated by Lord Moulton in *Helibut, Symons Ltd v*

Buckleton (1913) 'Not only the terms of such contracts, but the existence of an *animus contrahendi* on the part of all parties to them must be strictly shown'.

Identification of express terms

- See 'Incorporation of Terms' – Exemption Clauses.

Interpretation of express terms of a contract

Oral contracts
The contents is a matter of evidence for the judge. The interpretation will be undertaken by applying the objective rule (*Thake v Maurice* (1986)).

Written contracts
If a contract is reduced to writing then under the 'parol evidence' rule, oral or other evidence extrinsic to the document is not normally admissible to 'add to, vary, or contradict', the terms of the written agreement.

Exceptions
- to show that the contract is not legally binding, eg because of mistake or misrepresentation;

- to show that the contract is subject to a 'condition precedent'. *In Pym v Campbell* (1856) oral evidence was admitted to show that a contract was not to come into operation unless a patent was approved by a third party;

- to establish a custom or trade usage (*Hutton v Warren* (1836) see below);

- to establish that the written contract is not the whole contract. It is presumed that 'a document which looks like a contract is the whole contract', but this is rebuttable. See

Couchman v Hill (1947) and *Evans v Andrea Merzario* (above).

- A contract may be contained in more than one document (*Jacobs v Batavia Plantation Trust Ltd* (1924)).

- To establish a collateral contract (*City of Westminster Properties Ltd v Mudd* (1959) *Evans & Son Ltd v Andrea Merzario Ltd* (1976)) see above on collateral contracts.

The Law Commission recommended in 1976 that the 'Parol Evidence' rule be abolished. However, in view of the wide exceptions to the rule, it recommended in 1986 that no action need be taken.

Identification of implied terms

In addition to the terms which the parties have expressly agreed, a court may be prepared to hold that other terms must be implied into the contract. Such terms may be implied by:

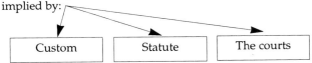

| Custom | Statute | The courts |

Custom

A contract may be deemed to incorporate any relevant custom of the market, trade or locality in which the contract is made. In *Hutton v Warren* (1836) a tenant established a right to fair allowance for improvements to the land through a local custom.

Statute

Parliament, as a matter of public policy, has in numerous instances, seen fit to imply terms into contracts, eg

> The Sale of Goods Act 1979 which implies the following terms into contracts for the sale of goods.

Terms implied into all sales:

- That the seller has the right to sell the goods;

- That goods sold by description correspond with the description.

Terms implied only into sales by way of business:

- That the goods are of satisfactory quality.

  Goods are of a satisfactory quality if they meet the standard that a reasonable person would regard as satisfactory, taking account of any description of the goods, the price, if relevant, and all other relevant circumstances, in particular their

  - ○ fitness for all purposes for which goods of that kind are commonly supplied,

  - ○ appearance and finish,

  - ○ freedom from minor defects,

  - ○ safety, and

  - ○ durability.

  It does not cover matters specifically drawn to the buyer's attention before the contract is made or, where the buyer examines the goods, defects which that examination should have revealed.

- That the goods are fit for any special purpose made known to the seller;

- That goods sold by sample correspond with the sample.

> The Supply of Goods and Services Act 1982
> implies similar terms into contracts of hire,
> contracts for work and materials, and other
> contracts not covered by the Sale of Goods Act.

- In contracts of service, there is an implied term that the service will be carried out with reasonable care and skill, within a reasonable time and for a reasonable price.

In *Wilson v Best* (1993) it was held that the duty of a travel agent under this provision extended to checking that the local safety regulations had been complied with. It did not require them to ensure that they complied with UK regulations.

> The Consumer Credit Act 1974.

The courts

| Terms implied in fact | Terms implied in law |

Terms implied in fact

When interpreting terms implied in fact – the court seeks to give effect to the unexpressed intention of the parties. There are two tests. A term may be implied because:

- It is necessary to give business efficacy to the contract. In *The Moorcock* (1889) a term was implied that the riverbed was in a condition that would not damage a ship unloading at the jetty.

- It satisfies the 'officious bystander' test, ie if a bystander suggested a term, the parties would respond with a common 'of course'. In *Spring v NASDS* (1956) the union tried to imply the 'Bridlington Agreement'. The court refused on the basis that if an 'officious bystander had suggested this, the plaintiff would have replied "What's that?"'

The *Moorcock* doctrine is used in order to make the contract workable, or where it was so obvious that the parties must have intended it to apply to the agreement. It will not be used merely because it was reasonable or because it would improve the contract.

It was suggested in *Shell UK Ltd v Lostock Garages Ltd* (1977) that the courts are reluctant to imply a term where the parties have entered into a detailed and carefully drafted written agreement.

Terms implied in law

- When terms are implied in law, they are implied into all contracts of a particular kind. Here the court is not trying to put into effect the parties intention, but is imposing an obligation on one party, often as a matter of public policy, eg the court implies into all contracts of employment a term that the employee will carry out his work with reasonable care and skill and will indemnify his employer against any loss caused by his negligence (*Lister v Romford Ice Cold Storage Co* (1957)).

- In these cases, the implication is not based on the presumed intention of the parties, but on the court's perception of the nature of the relationship between the parties, and whether such an implied term was reasonable.

- In *Liverpool CC v Irwin* (1977) the tenants of a block of council flats failed to persuade the court to imply a term that the council should be responsible for the common parts of the building on the *Moorcock* or 'officious bystander' test, but succeeded on the basis of the *Lister* test, ie the term should be implied in law in that the agreement was incomplete, it involved the relationship of landlord and tenant and it would be reasonable to expect the landlord to be responsible for the common parts of the building.

Classification of terms

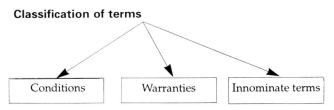

There is a very important distinction between those terms of a contract which entitle an innocent party to terminate (rescind or treat as discharged) a contract in the event of a breach, and those which merely enable a person to claim damages.

Traditionally, a distinction has been made in English law between:

Conditions

> Statements of fact or promises which form the essential terms of the contract. If the statement is not true, or the promise is not fulfilled, the injured party may terminate (or treat as discharged) the contract and claim damages.

- The SGA 1979 designates certain implied terms, eg re satisfactory quality as conditions – the breach of which entitles the buyer to terminate (or treat as discharged) the contract.

- In *Poussard v Spiers & Pond* (1876) a singer failed to take up a role in an opera until a week after the season had started. Held – her promise to perform as from the first performance was a condition – and its breach entitled the management to treat the contract as discharged.

Warranties

> Contractual terms concerning the less important or subsidiary statements of facts or promises. If a warranty is broken, this does not entitle the other party to terminate (or treat as discharged) the contract, it merely entitles him to sue for damages.

- The SGA 1979 designates certain terms as warranties, breach of which do not allow the buyer to treat the contract as discharged, but merely to sue for damages, eg the right to quiet enjoyment.

- In *Bettini v Gye* (1876) a singer was engaged to sing for a whole season and to arrive six days in advance to take part in rehearsals. He only arrived three days in advance. Held – the rehearsal clause was subsidiary to the main clause. It was only a warranty. The management was therefore not entitled to treat the contract as discharged, they should have kept to the original contract and sought damages for the three days delay.

Innominate or intermediate terms

- In the *Hong Kong Fir Shipping Co v Kawasaki Kisen Kaisha* (1962) it was suggested by the Court of Appeal that it was not enough to classify terms into conditions and warranties. Regard should also be had to the character and nature of the breach itself. Innominate or intermediate terms were discussed. In *Hong Kong Fir* the defendants chartered the vessel Hong Kong Fir for the plaintiffs for 24 months; the charter party provided that 'she being fitted in every way for ordinary cargo service'. The vessel spent less than nine weeks of the first seven months at sea because of breakdowns and the consequent repairs which were necessary.

> Held – the terms was neither a condition nor a warranty, and in determining whether the defendants could terminate the contract, it was necessary to look at the consequences of the breach to see if it deprived the innocent party of substantially the whole benefit he should have received under the contract.

On the facts, this was not the case because the charter party still had a substantial time to run.

After the *Hong Kong Fir* case in 1962, there was some confusion as to whether the breach based test which applied to innominate terms had replaced the term based test which relied on the distinction between conditions and warranties or merely added to it an alternative in certain circumstances.

- In the *Mihalis Angelos* (1970) the Court of Appeal reverted to the term based test. The owners of a vessel stated that the vessel was 'expected ready to load' on or about 1 July. It was discovered that this was not so. Held – the term was a condition – the charterers could treat the contract as discharged.

In 1976, two cases were decided on the breach based principle.

- In *Cehave v Bremer Handelsgesellshaft MBH, The Hansa Nord* (1976) the seller had sold a cargo of citrus pellets with a term in the contract that the shipment be made in good condition. The buyer rejected the cargo on the basis that this term has been broken. The defect, however, was not serious, and the court held that although the Sale of Goods Act had classified some terms as conditions and warranties, it did not follow that all the terms had to be so classified. Accordingly, the court could consider the effect of the breach, since this was not serious, the buyer had not been entitled to reject.

- In *Reardon Smith v Hansen Tangen* (1976) an oil tanker was described as 'Osaka No 354', where in fact it was 'Oshine No 004', but was otherwise exactly as specified. Because the market for oil tankers had collapsed the charterers sought to argue that the number was a condition which would enable them to repudiate the contract. The House of Lords rejected this argument. Held – the statement was an innominate term, not a condition – since the effect of the breach was trivial and did not justify termination of the contract.

The relationship, between the two tests, the term based test and the breach based test was explained by the House of Lords in *Bunge Corpn v Tradax* (1981). On the facts of this case the House of Lords held that stipulations with regard to time will generally be held to be conditions in a mercantile contract and the innocent party could treat the contract as discharged if the condition was not complied with. Their Lordships stated that:

> If a term is a condition, then breach of that term will allow the other party to treat the contract as discharged.

- Note, the time for determining whether a clause was a condition or an innominate term is at the time of contracting – not after the breach.

Traditionally, a term is a condition if it has been established as such.

- By statute – eg the Sale of Goods Act 1979.

- By precedent after a judicial decision. In *The Mihalis Angelos* (1970) the Court of Appeal held that the 'expected readiness' clause in a charter party is a condition.

- By the intention of the parties. The court must ascertain the intention of the parties. If the wording clearly reveals that the parties intended that breach of a particular term should give rise to a right to rescind – that term will be regarded as a condition. In *Lombard North Central v Butterworth* (1987) the Court of Appeal held that contracting parties can provide expressly in the contract that 'specific breaches could terminate the contract'. In that case, the contract included an express clause that the time for payment of instalments was 'of the essence of the contract'. An accountant had agreed to hire a computer for five years, agreeing to make an initial payment and 19 quarterly rental payments. He was late in paying some instalments, and the owners terminated the agreement, recovered possession of the computer, and claimed damages not only for the arrears, but also for loss of future instalments. The claim succeeded because the contract specifically stated that the time of payment of each instalment was to be of the essence of the contract.

Note, the mere use of the word 'condition' is not conclusive.

In *Schuler v Wickman Tool Sales Ltd* (1974) the House of Lords held that breach of a 'condition' that a distributor should visit six customers a week could not have been intended to allow rescission. The word 'condition' had not been used in this particular sense. There was in the contract a separate clause which indicated when and how the contract could be terminated.

- By the court – deciding according to the subject matter of the contract (see *Poussard v Spiers* (1876) and *Bettini v Gye* (1876) above).

> If a term is not a condition, then the 'wait and see' technique can be used to decide if the gravity of the breach is such that it deprived the innocent party of substantially the whole benefit of the contract. If so – then the innocent party can terminate the contract (innominate or intermediate term).

Certainty and flexibility

Certainty

- The term based test is alleged to have the advantage of predictability and certainty. It is important for the parties to know their legal rights and liabilities as regards the availability of termination. The character of all terms is ascertainable at the moment the contract is concluded. Nothing that happens after its formation can change the status of a term. If the term is a condition – then the parties will know that its breach allows the other party to terminate, eg where the term is designated a condition be it by legislation or by precedent or by the parties themselves. But there can still be uncertainty where the parties have to await the court's decision on the nature of the term.

- The advantage of certainty is however balanced by the fact that it is possible to terminate a contract on a technicality, for sometimes a very minor breach.

Flexibility

- The breach based test is stated to bring flexibility to the law. Instead of saying that the innocent party can, in the case of a condition, always terminate or in the case of a warranty, never terminate, innominate terms allow the courts to permit termination where the circumstances justify it and the consequences are sufficiently serious.

- It is, however, more difficult for the innocent party to know when he has the right to terminate, or for the party in breach to realise in advance the consequence of his action.

> Note, the distinction between the different types of contract terms remains of considerable importance.

4 Exemption (exclusion or limitation) clauses

> A clause which purports to exclude, wholly or in part, liability for the happening of certain events.

A total exclusion is referred to as an exclusion clause; a partial exclusion is known as a limitation clause.

Exemption clauses are most commonly found in standard form contracts.

To be valid, an exemption clause must satisfy the tests set by the

| Common law | Unfair Contract Terms Act 1977 | Regulations on Unfair Terms in Consumer Contracts 1995 |

Common law requirements

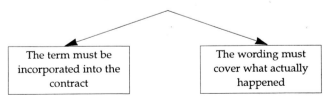

| The term must be incorporated into the contract | The wording must cover what actually happened |

Incorporation

- This requirement applies to all terms; but has been interpreted strictly in the case of exemption clauses.

A term may be incorporated into a contract by being

Contained in a signed document
In *L'Éstrange v Graucob Ltd* (1934) the plaintiff had signed a contract of sale without reading it. Held – she was bound by the terms which contained an exemption clause.

Exceptions
Where the offeree has been induced to sign as a result of misrepresentation.

- In *Curtis v Chemical Cleaning Co* (1951) the plaintiff signed a 'receipt' when she took a dress to be cleaned, on being told that it was to protect the cleaners in case of damage to the sequins. In fact the clause excluded liability for all damage. Held – the cleaners were not protected for damage to the dress, the extent of the clause had been misrepresented and therefore the cleaners could not rely on it.

- '*Non est factum*' (see Chapter 5).

Contained in an unsigned document (ticket cases)
- This must be seen to be a contractual document.

   ○ In *Chapelton v Barry UDC* (1940), on hiring a deck chair, the plaintiff was given a ticket with only a large black 3d on the face of the ticket, and exclusion clauses on the back. Held – the defendants could not rely on the exclusion clauses as it was not apparent on the face of it that the ticket was a contractual document, rather than just a receipt.

- Reasonable notice of the term must be given.

  ○ In *Parker v South Eastern Railway Co* (1877) the plaintiff received a ticket which stated on the face 'see back'. Held – the plaintiff was bound by an exemption clause printed on the back although he had not read it because the railway company had given reasonable notice of its existence. Notice can be reasonable although it refers to other documents.

  ○ In *Thompson v London Midland and Scottish Railway* (1930) the ticket indicated that the conditions of the contract could be seen at the station masters office, or on the timetable. The exemption clause was in clause 552 of the timetable which cost 6d – the ticket itself only cost 2/6.

  ○ The test is objective, and it is irrelevant that the party affected by the exemption clause is blind or illiterate, or otherwise unable to understand it (*Thompson v LMS* above).

  ○ But in *Geir v Kujawa* (1970) a notice in English was stuck on the windscreen of a car stating that passengers travelled at their own risk. A German passenger who was known to speak no English was held not to be bound by the clause as reasonable care had not been taken to bring it to his attention.

- Attention must be drawn to any unusual clause.

  ○ In *Thornton v Shoe Lane Parking* (1971) it was stated that a person who drives his car into a car park might expect to find in his contract a clause excluding liability for loss or damage to the car; but special notice should have been given of a clause purporting to exclude liability for personal injury.

○ In *Interfoto Picture Library v Stiletto Visual Programmes* (1989) the Court of Appeal confirmed that onerous conditions required special measures to bring them to the attention of the defendant. The clause in that case was not an exemption clause, but a clause imposing retention charges 10 times higher than normal. The Court of Appeal stated, the more unusual the clause, the greater the notice required.

- Notice of the term must be communicated to the other party before, or at the time that, the contract is entered into.

  ○ In *Thornton v Shoe Lane Parking Ltd* (1971) the plaintiff made his contract with the car company when he inserted a coin in the ticket machine. The ticket was issued afterwards, and in any case referred to conditions displayed inside the car park which he could see only after entry.

- The rules of offer and acceptance, and the distinctions between offers and invitations to treat must be consulted in order to ascertain when the contract was made. Problems with regard to incorporation can arise in a typical 'Battle of the Forms' problem. See *Butler Machine Tool Ltd v Ex-Cell-O Corpn* (Chapter 1).

Notice by display

Notices exhibited in premises seeking to exclude liability for loss or damage, are common, eg 'car parked at owner's risk' and must be seen before, or at the time of entry into contract.

- In *Olley v Marlborough Court Hotel* (1949) Mr and Mrs Olley saw a notice on the hotel bedroom wall which stated 'the proprietors will not hold themselves responsible for articles lost or stolen, unless handed to the manageress for safe-keeping'. The defendants were liable only after the contract had been entered into and it was therefore not incorporated into the contract and would not protect the proprietors.

Notice by a 'course of dealing'

- If there has been a course of dealing between the parties, the usual terms may be incorporated into the contract although not specifically drawn to the attention of the parties at the time the contract was entered into.

In *Spurling v Bradshaw* (1956) Bradshaw deposited some orange juice in Spurling's warehouse. The contractual document excluding liability for loss or damage was not sent to Spurling until several days after the contract. Held – the exclusion clauses were valid, as the parties had always done business with each other on this basis.

- Note, the transactions must be sufficiently numerous to constitute a course of dealings. The established course of dealings must be consistent. The established course of dealings must not have been deviated from on the occasion in question.

In *Hollier v Rambler Motors* (1972) the Court of Appeal held that bringing a car to be serviced or repaired at a garage on three or four occasions over a period of five years did not establish a course of dealings.

Notice through patent knowledge

- In *British Crane Hire Corpn v Ipswich Plant Hire* (1975) the owner of a crane hired it out to a contractor who was also engaged in the same business. It was held that the hirer was bound by the owner's usual terms though they were not actually communicated at the time of the contract.

They were, however, based on a model supplied by a trade association, to which both parties belonged. It was stated that they were reasonable, and were well known in the trade.

Oral contracts

- Whether a clause has been incorporated into an oral contract is a matter of evidence for the court (*McCutcheon v MacBrayne* (1964)).

On a proper construction, the clause covers the loss in question

- An exclusion clause is interpreted *contra preferentem*, ie any ambiguity in the clause will be interpreted against the party seeking to rely on it.

  ○ In *Houghton v Trafalgar Insurance Co Ltd* (1954) it was held that the word 'load' could not refer to people.

  ○ In *Andrews Bros v Singer & Co Ltd* (1934) an exclusion referring to implied terms was not allowed to cover a term that the car was new, as this was an express term.

  It was suggested by the House of Lords in *Photo Production Ltd v Securicor Ltd* (1980) that any need for a strained and distorted interpretation of the English language has been banished by the UCTA.

- Especially clear words must be used in order to exclude liability for negligence, eg the use of the word 'negligence', or the phrase 'howsoever caused' (*Smith v South Wales Switchgear Ltd* (1978)).

  But if these words are not used, provided the wording is wide enough to cover negligence, and there is no other liability to which they can apply then it is assumed that they must have been intended to cover negligence (*Canada Steamship Lines v The King* (1952)).

- It was stated in *Ailsa Craig Fishing Co v Malvern Fishing Co* (1983) that limitation clauses may be interpreted less rigidly than exclusion clauses.

- Only a party to a contract can rely on an exclusion clause. (See Chapter 10.)

- Especially clear words are required when the breach is of a fundamental nature. In the past, Lord Denning and others argued that it was not possible to exclude breaches of contract which were deemed to be fundamental by any exclusion clause, however widely and clearly drafted. (Rule of Law approach).

However, The House of Lords confirmed in *Photo Production Ltd v Securicor Ltd* (1980) that the doctrine of fundamental breach was a rule of construction not a rule of law, ie liability for a fundamental breach could be excluded, if the words were sufficiently clear and precise.

The House also stated that:

- The decision in *Harbutt's Plasticine Ltd v Wayne Tank and Pump Co* (1970) was not good law. In that case the Court of Appeal had held that as a fundamental breach brought a contract to an end there was no exclusion clause left to protect the perpetrator of the breach.

- That there is no difference between a 'fundamental term' and a 'condition'.

- A strained construction should not be put on words in an exclusion clause which are clearly and fairly susceptible to only one meaning.

○ Where the parties are bargaining on equal terms, they should be free to apportion risks as they wish.

○ The courts should be wary of interfering with the settled practices of business men, as an exclusion clause often serves to identify who should insure against a particular loss.

Unfair Contract Terms Act 1977

Note, the title is misleading.

- The Act does not cover all unfair contract terms, only exemption clauses.

- The Act covers certain tortious liability, as well as contractual liability. The following must be examined.

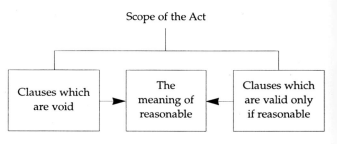

Scope of the Act

Scope of the Act

- s 1 – the Act applies to contracts made after 1 February 1978 which arise in the course of business. 'Business' includes a profession and the activities of any government department, and/or public or local authority.

- s 5 – contracts specifically excluded include contracts of insurance, contracts for the transfer of land and international commercial contracts.

- s 13 – the Act limits the effectiveness of clauses that exclude or restrict liability. It also covers clauses which make it difficult to enforce a contract, eg restrictive time limits; or exclude particular remedies; in *Stewart Gill v Horatio Myer and Co* (1992), it was held that a clause restricting a right of set-off or counterclaim was subject to the act. It was also held in *Smith v Bush* (1990) that it covered 'disclaimers which restrictively defined a party's obligation under a contract'. In that case a valuation was stated to be given 'without any acceptance of liability for its accuracy'.

Negligence

- The Act covers contractual, tortious and statutory negligence.

- The difference between excluding liability for negligence, and transferring liability for negligence is seen in *Phillips Products v Hyland Bros* (1987) where the contract transferred liability for the negligence of the driver of a hired excavator to the hirer. The driver negligently damaged property belonging to the hirer. Held the clause was an exclusion clause and was subject to UCTA. The hirer had no-one to sue.

- In *Thompson v Lohan (Plant Hire)* (1987) on the other hand an excavator and driver were hired under the same conditions. The driver negligently killed a third party. Held – the clause transferring liability to the hirer was not an exclusion clause in this case as the third party was able to sue the hirer. It was merely a clause transferring liability.

Misrepresentation

- The difference between excluding liability for misrepresentation, and defining the powers of an agent is seen in *Cremdean Properties v Nash* (1977) where a clause in the special conditions of sale stating that the 'particulars were believed to be correct, but their accuracy is not guaranteed' was held to be an exclusion clause.

- In *Collins v Howell Jones* (1980) however, the Court of Appeal held a statement that the 'vendor does not make or give any representation or warranty and neither the estate agent or any person in their employment has any authority to make or give a representation or warranty whatsoever in relation to the property' had the effect of defining or limiting the scope of the agent's authority.

Effect of the Act

Clauses which are void
Exclusions of liability:

- For death or personal injury caused by negligence (s 2).

- In a manufacturer's guarantee for loss or damage caused by negligence (s 5).

- For the statutory guarantee of title in contracts for the sale of goods or hire-purchase (s 6).

- For the other statutory guarantees in contracts for the sale of goods and hire-purchase in consumer contracts (description, satisfactory quality, fitness for purpose) (s 6).

- For similar statutory guarantees in other consumer contracts for the supply of goods, eg contracts of hire (s 7).

Clauses which are valid only if reasonable

Clauses excluding liability:

- For loss or damage to property caused by negligence (s 2).

- For breach of contract in a consumer or standard form contract (s 3). Also clauses claiming to render a substantially different performance from that reasonably expected, or to render no performance at all (s 3).

- For statutory guarantees (other than those concerning title) contracts for the sale of goods and hire-purchase (description, satisfactory quality, and fitness for purpose) in inter-business contracts (s 6).

- For statutory guarantees concerning title or possession in other contracts for the supply of goods (eg hire) (s 7).

- For other statutory guarantees (description, satisfactory quality, fitness for purpose) in other contracts for the supply of goods in inter-business contracts (s 7).

- For misrepresentation in all contracts.

Note

'Consumer transaction' – a person is a 'consumer' where he does not make or hold himself out as making the contract in the course of business, and the other party does make the contract in the course of business. In contracts for the sale of goods – the goods must also be of a type normally sold for private use.

- A controversial interpretation of a 'consumer' was made by the Court of Appeal in *R&B Customs v United Dominion Trust* (1988) where a car was bought by a private company for the business and private use of its directors. It was held by the Court of Appeal that it was not bought 'in the course of a business'. Buying cars was incidental, not central to the business of the company. If it is incidental only, then the purchase would only be 'in the course of a business' if it was one made with sufficient regularity.

A 'standard from transaction' occurs when the parties deal on the basis of a standard form provided by one of them.

Reasonableness

> It is for the person relying on the
> clause to prove that the clause is reasonable.

In assessing reasonability, the following matters should be considered.

Section 11 UCTA
- Contract terms are to be adjudged reasonable or not according to the circumstances which were, or ought reasonably to have been, known to the parties when the contract was made.

- Where a person seeks to restrict liability to a specified sum of money, regard should be had to the resources which he could expect to be available to him for the purpose of meeting the liability; and as to how far it was open to him to cover himself by insurance.

- In determining for the purpose of ss 6 or 7, whether a contract term satisfies the requirement of reasonableness, regard shall be had to the

  ○ the strength of the bargaining position of the parties relative to each other;

○ whether the customer received an inducement to agree to the term and had an opportunity of entering into a similar contract with other persons but without having to accept similar terms;

○ whether the customer knew, or ought reasonably to have known of the existence and extent of the term;

○ where the exclusion is conditional, whether it was reasonable to expect that compliance with that condition would be practicable;

○ whether the goods were manufactured, processed, or adapted to the special order of the customer (Schedule 2).

Decisions of the courts

In *Smith v Bush* (1990) and *Harris v Wyre Forest DC* (1989) the House of Lords dealt with two cases involving the validity of an exclusion clause protecting surveyors who had carried out valuations of a house. The House of Lords decided that the clauses were exclusion clauses designed to protect the surveyors against claims for negligence. Lord Griffiths declared that there were four matters which should always be considered:

• Were the parties of equal bargaining power?

• In the case of advice, would it have been reasonable to obtain advice from another source?

• Was the task being undertaken a difficult one, for which the protection of an exclusion clause was necessary?

• What would be the practical consequences for the parties of the decision on reasonableness? For example, would the defendant normally be insured? Would the plaintiff have to bear the cost himself?

In inter-business contracts, the practices of businessmen are considered.

- In *Photo Production v Securicor* (1980) the House of Lords stated that the courts should be reluctant to interfere with the settled practices of businesses. They pointed out that the function of an exclusion clause was often to indicate who should insure against a particular risk.

- In *Green v Cade Bros* (1983) it was decided that a clause requiring notice of rejection within three days of delivery of seed potatoes was unreasonable, as a defect could not have been discovered by inspection within this time, but a clause limiting damages to the contract price was upheld – as it had been negotiated by organisations representing the buyers and sellers, and 'certified' potatoes had been available for a small extra charge (ie Schedule 2 above was applied).

- However, in *George Mitchel v Finney Lock Seeds Ltd* (1983) the buyers suffered losses of £61,000, due to the supply of the wrong variety of cabbage seeds. The contract limited the liability of the seller to a refund of the price paid (£192). Held – the clause was not reasonable. Matters taken into consideration:

  ○ the clause was inserted unilaterally – there was no negotiation;

  ○ loss was caused by the negligence of the seller;

  ○ the seller could have insured against his liability;

  ○ the sellers implied that they themselves considered the clause unreasonable by accepting liability in previous cases.

The availability of insurance seems important in all cases.

Regulations on unfair terms in consumer contracts

| Coverage | Fairness | Remedies |

- Based on EU Directive on Unfair Terms in Consumer Contracts.

Coverage
- The regulations will apply to:

> 'any term in a contract between
> a seller or supplier and a consumer where
> the term has not been individually negotiated'
> ie it has been drafted in advance.

This will be so, even if some other parts of the contract have not been drafted in advance.

- The regulations will not apply to contracts which relate to employment, family law, or succession rights, companies or partnerships terms included in order to comply with legislation or an international convention.

- It does however, cover insurance policies and contracts relating to land.

- A 'business' is defined to include a trade or profession and the activities of any government department or local or public authority.

- A 'consumer' means a natural person who is acting for a purpose outside his business.

Note, it is wider than UCTA in that it covers all terms not only exclusion clauses, eg harsh terms concerning unauthorised overdrafts. It is narrower than UCTA in that it only covers clauses in consumer contracts which have not been individually negotiated. The definition of a consumer is also narrower *cf R&B Customs v UDT* (1988).

Unfairness

> The clause is unfair if, contrary to the requirements of good faith, it creates a significant imbalance in the parties' rights and obligations, to the detriment of the consumer.

Regard must be had to the nature of the goods and services provided, the other terms of the contract and all the circumstances relating to its conclusion.

The definition of the main subject matter and the adequacy of the price or remuneration are not relevant.

In assessing good faith, attention should be paid to

- the strength of the parties;

- whether the consumer had an inducement to agree to the term;

- whether the goods or services were sold or supplied to the special order of the consumer;

- the extent to which the seller or supplier had dealt fairly and equitably with the consumer;

- indicative and non-exhaustive list of terms which may be unfair is included;

- the term should be expressed in plain English, and any ambiguity should be interpreted in the customer's favour.

Effect of an unfair term

- The term itself shall not be binding on the consumer, but the rest of the contract may be enforced.

- The Director General of Fair Trading will have a duty to consider any complaint made to him that a term is unfair. Where appropriate he must seek an injunction to bar the use of the term not only in a particular contract but also in similar contracts and also contracts issued by trade associations.

5 Vitiating elements which render a contract voidable

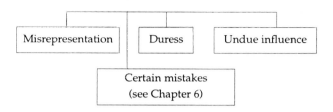

Significance of a contract being voidable

> The innocent party may set the contract aside,
> if he so wishes.

Thus:

- The innocent party may, if he wishes, affirm the contract.

- Where the innocent party has not performed the contract, he may refuse to perform and rely on the misrepresentation as a defence.

- The misled party may rescind the contract by:

  ○ informing the other party; or

  ○ where a fraudulent party cannot be traced, by informing the police (*Car & Universal Finance Co v Caldwell* (1965)); or

  ○ bringing legal proceedings.

- It was stated in *TSB v Camfield* (1995) that the right to rescind is that of the representee not the court. All the court can do is decide whether the representee has lawfully exercised the right to rescind. It is not therefore an exercise of equitable relief by the court.

Rescission

> Restoring the parties as far as is possible
> to the position they were in before they entered
> into the contract.

- But in *Cheese v Thomas* (1993) the court declared that the court must look at all the circumstances to do what was 'fair and just'. In that case a house which had been jointly bought had to be sold afterwards at a considerable loss. The agreement between the two parties for the purchase of the house was rescinded, but the court held that it was not necessary for the guilty party to bear the whole of the loss. It was fair and just that the proceeds should be divided according to their respective contributions.

- This contrasts with the normal situation where a property has diminished in value, and the misled party would get all his money returned (*Erlanger v New Sombrero Phosphate Co* (1878)).

- As part of this restoration, equity may order a sum of money to be paid to the misled person to indemnify him against any obligations necessarily created by the contract.

In *Whittington v Seale-Hayne* (1900) the plaintiffs, breeders of prize poultry, were induced to take a lease of the defendants premises by his innocent misrepresentation that the premises were in a sanitary condition. Under the lease, the plaintiffs covenanted to execute all works required by any local or public authority. Owing to the insanitary conditions of the premises, the water supply was poisoned, the plaintiffs' manager and his family became very ill, and the poultry became valueless for breeding purposes or died. In addition, the local authority required the drains to be renewed. The plaintiffs sought an indemnity for all his losses. The court rescinded the lease, and held that the plaintiffs could recover an indemnity for what they had spent on rates, rent and repairs under the covenants in the lease, because these expenses arose necessarily out of the contract. It refused to award compensation for other losses, since to do so would be to award damages, not an indemnity, there being no obligation created by the contract to carry on a poultry farm on the premises or to employ a manager etc.

- Note, rescission, even if enforced by the court, is always the act of the defrauded party. It is effective from the date it is communicated to the representor or the police (see above) and not from the date of any judgment in subsequent litigation.

Rescission is subject to certain bars

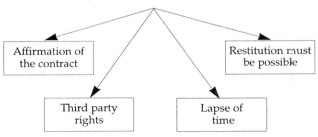

| Affirmation of the contract | | Restitution must be possible |
| Third party rights | | Lapse of time |

Affirmation of the contract

The representee may not rescind if he has affirmed the contract after learning of the misrepresentation either by declaring his intention to proceed with the contract or by performing some act from which such an intention can be inferred. In *Long v Lloyd* (1958) the buyer of a lorry undertook a long journey after discovering serious defects in the lorry. Held – he had affirmed the contract.

Lapse of time

This can provide evidence of affirmation where the misrepresentee fails to rescind for a considerable time after discovering the falsity.

In cases of innocent misrepresentation lapse of time can operate as a separate bar to rescission. In *Leaf v International Galleries* (1950) the plaintiff bought a picture which the seller had innocently misrepresented to be by Constable. Five years later the plaintiff discovered it was not by Constable and immediately sought to rescind the contract. Held – barred by lapse of time.

Restitution must be possible

A person seeking to rescind the contract must be able and willing to restore what he has received under it. However, rescission is an equitable remedy, and the court will not allow minor failures in the restoration to the original position to stand in the way. In *Erlanger v New Sombrero Phosphate Co* (1878) the purchaser had worked phosphate mines briefly. Held – he could rescind by restoring property and accounting for any profit derived from it.

Third Party Rights

There can be no rescission if third parties have acquired rights in the subject matter of the contract. See *Phillips v Brooks* (1919) and *Lewis v Averay* (1972) – Chapter 6.

Misrepresentation

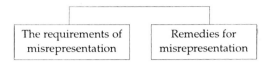

| The requirements of misrepresentation | Remedies for misrepresentation |

Representations and terms of a contract

Material statements made during negotiations leading to a contact may be either:

- Terms of the contract. If these are untrue, the untruth constitutes a breach of contract.

- Statements which helped to induce the contract, ie 'mere representations'. If untrue – they are 'misrepresentations'.

(For distinctions between terms and 'mere representations' – see Chapter 3.)

Requirements of misrepresentation

It must be:

> An untrue statement of fact made by one party to the contract (representor) to the other (representee) which induces the other to enter into the contract.

A statement of fact

- Not a 'mere puff', ie a statement so vague as to be without effect, eg describing a house as a 'desirable residence'.

- Not a promise. A promise to do something in the future is only actionable if the promise amounts to a binding contract (*Kleinwort Benson Ltd v Malaysian Mining Corpn Bhd* (1989)).

- Not a statement of opinion, eg in *Bisset v Wilkinson* (1927) the vendor of a farm which had never been used as a sheep farm stated that in his judgment the farm would support 2,000 sheep. Held – a statement of opinion.

  But a statement expressed as an opinion may be treated as a statement of fact if the person making the statement was in a position to know the true facts. In *Smith v Land & House Prop Corp* (1884) the vendor of a hotel described it as 'let to a most desirable tenant', when the tenant had for a long time been in arrears with the rent. The Court of Appeal held there was a misrepresentation of fact.

- Not a statement of intention. But if the representor did not have that intention, then it is a misstatement of fact as in *Edgington v Fitzmaurice* (1885) where the directors issued a prospectus claiming that the money raised was to be used to improve the company's buildings and to expand its business. Their real intention was to pay off the company's debts. Held – fraudulent misrepresentation.

- Not a statement of law.

An active representation
- The statement will normally be in words, but other forms of communication which misrepresent the facts will suffice, as in *Horsfall v Thomas* (1862) (below).

- Failure to make a statement, however, non-disclosure of facts – will not generally qualify as misrepresentation.

Exceptions
- Where facts have been selected to give a misleading impression as in *Dimmock v Hallett* (1866) where a vendor of

land stated that farms were let, but omitted to say that the tenants had given notice to quit.

- Where circumstances have changed since a representation was made, then the representor has a duty to correct the statement. In *With v O'Flanagan* (1936) it was stated correctly that a medical practice was worth £2,000 a year, but by the time the practice changed hands, it was practically worthless. Held – there was a duty to disclose the changed circumstances.

- Contracts *ubberrimae fideii* ('of the utmost good faith'), eg

  ○ Contract of Insurance. Material facts must be disclosed, ie facts which would influence an insurer in deciding whether to accept the proposal, or to fix the amount of the premium, eg a policy of life insurance has been avoided because it was not disclosed that the proposer had already been turned down by other insurers.

  ○ Family arrangements. In *Gordon v Gordon* (1816–19) a division of property based on the proposition that the elder son was illegitimate was set aside upon proof that the younger son had concealed his knowledge of a private marriage ceremony solemnised before the birth of this brother.

  ○ Analogous contracts. Where there is a duty to disclose, not material, but unusual facts, eg contracts of suretyship.

It must have been a material inducement

A statement likely to induce a person to contract will normally be assumed to have done so. There is no inducement, however, where:

- The misrepresentee or his agent actually knew the truth.

- Where the misrepresentee was ignorant of the misrepresentation when the contract was made. In *Horsfall v Thomas* (1862) the vendor of a gun concealed a defect in the gun (misrepresentation by conduct). The buyer, however, bought the gun without examining it. Held – the attempted misrepresentation had not induced the contract.

- The misrepresentee did not allow the representation to affect his judgment. In *Attwood v Small* (1838) a buyer appointed an agent to check the statement made by the seller as to the reserves in a mine. Held – not actionable misrepresentation. The buyer had relied on his own agents statements, not that of the vendor.

- Provided that the representation was one of the inducements, it need not be the sole inducement.

- The fact that the representee did not take advantage of an opportunity to check the statement is no bar to an action for misrepresentation.

  In *Redgrave v Hurd* (1881) a solicitor was induced to purchase a house and practice by the innocent misrepresentation of the seller. Held – he was entitled to rescission although he did not examine the documents which were available to him and which would have indicated to him the true state of affairs.

- Neither is it contributory negligence not to check a statement made by a vendor (*Gran Gelato v Richcliff* (1992)).

Remedies for misrepresentation

Rescission

Misrepresentation renders a contract voidable – see above. The Misrepresentation Act 1967 provides that rescission is available for:

- 'executed' contracts for the sale of goods and conveyances of property;

- representations which have been incorporated as a term of the contract;

Rescission was not available in these circumstances before 1967.

Damages

- There are five ways in which damages may be claimed for misrepresentation. It seems likely that in future the normal ground for damages will be the Misrepresentation Act 1967; but there are still cases where damages can only be claimed at common law, if at all.

- Note, rescission and damages are alternative remedies in many cases, but if the victim of fraudulent or negligent misrepresentation has suffered consequential loss he may rescind and sue for damages.

- Damages can be claimed on different bases, according to the kind of misrepresentation that was committed.

Damages in the tort of deceit for fraudulent misrepresentation

It is up to the misled party to prove that the misrepresentation was made fraudulently, ie knowingly, without belief in its truth, or recklessly, as to whether it be true or false (*Derry v Peek* (1889)).

The burden of proof on the misled party is a heavy one.

Damages in the tort on negligence

Victims of negligent misrepresentation may be able to sue under *Hedley Byrne v Heller & Partners* (1963). The misrepresentee must prove (1) that the misrepresentor owed him a duty to take reasonable care in making the representation, ie there must be a 'special relationship' (2) that the statement had been made negligently.

Damages under s 2(1) Misrepresentation Act 1967

Section 2(1) Misrepresentation Act 1967 provides that where a person has entered into a contract after a misrepresentation has been made to him by another party thereto, and as a result of it has suffered loss, 'then if the misrepresentor would be liable for damages if it had been made fraudulently, he will be so liable notwithstanding that the misrepresentation was not made fraudulently, unless he proves that he had reasonable grounds to believe, and did believe up to the time the contract was made that the facts represented were true'.

Note that this is a more beneficial remedy for the misrepresentee as he only need prove that the statement is untrue. It is for the misrepresentor to prove that he had good grounds for making the statement, and the burden of proof is a heavy one. In *Howard Marine and Dredging Co Ltd v Ogden* (1978) the owner of two barges told the hirer that the capacity of the barges was 1,600 tons. He obtained these figures from the Lloyds list, but in this case the Lloyds list was incorrect. The court held that he did not have good grounds for this statement; he should have consulted the manufacturer's specifications which should have been in his possession.

Assessment of damages

> Damages in the tort of deceit and the tort of negligence are assessed on the tortious basis of reliance, ie the plaintiff is entitled to be put in the position he was in before the tort was committed.

The Court of Appeal confirmed in *Royscot Trustv Rogerson* (1991) that damages under s 2(1) of the Misrepresentation Act should also be awarded on the reliance basis, because of the 'fiction of fraud' in the wording of the Act.

Remoteness of damage

The Court of Appeal also held in that case, because of the 'fiction of fraud' that the rules of remoteness which apply only to the tort of deceit should be applied

> ie damages would be awarded to cover all losses which flow directly from the the untrue statement, whether or not those losses were foreseeable.

(In contract and in all torts other than deceit the losses must be 'reasonably foreseeable'.)

- In *Royscot Trust v Rogerson* (1991) a customer arranged to acquire a car on hire-purchase from a car dealer. The finance was to be provided by a finance company, the Royscott Trust, which insisted on a deposit of 20%. The dealer falsified the figures in order to indicate a deposit of 20% as required. Some months later, the customer wrongfully sold the car, thus depriving the finance company of its property. The finance company sued the dealer under s 2(1) Misrepresentation Act. It was held by the Court of Appeal that the finance company could recover damages from the car dealer to cover the loss of the car, since the loss followed the misrepresentation, the remoteness rules applicable to the tort of deceit would be applied and the loss did not need to be foreseeable.

Controversy has followed this decision, as the tort of deceit to which this rule only previously applied is difficult to establish and involves moral culpability on the part of the defendant. It has now been extended to an action which is relatively easy to establish (see *Howard Marine and Dredging v Ogden*) and may only involve carelessness.

- Further problems are caused by the decision of the Court of Appeal in *East v Maurer* (1991) a case in the tort of deceit where it was held that 'all damages flowing directly from the fraud' would cover damages for loss of profit – a heading previously considered to be appropriate only to expectation damages in contract. It is a matter for speculation whether the courts will apply this decision to cases under the Misrepresentation Act and cover loss of profit under the heading of reliance loss on the basis that all losses which flow directly from the misrepresentation will be recoverable.

- A generous interpretation of s 2(1) Misrepresentation Act 1967 had also been applied by the court in *Naughton v O'Callaghan* (1990) where reliance damages had been awarded to cover not only the difference between the value of the colt and the value it would have had if the statements made about it were correct (the quantification rule for breach of contract); but also the cost of its maintenance since the sale.

It has been alleged that these three cases swell the amount of damages which can be awarded under the Misrepresentation Act to a greater extent than that intended by Parliament, and that the damages available for misrepresentation can now exceed those available for breach of contract.

Damages for wholly innocent misrepresentation

Damages cannot be claimed for a misrepresentation which is not fraudulent or negligent, but

- an indemnity may be awarded (see above);

- damages in lieu of rescission may be awarded under s 2(2) Misrepresentation Act 1967;

  in *William Sindal v Cambridgeshire CC* (1994) the Court of Appeal stated (*obiter*) that where the court is considering whether to award damages in lieu of rescission, three matters should be taken into consideration:

  ○ the nature of the misrepresentation;

  ○ the loss which would be caused to the representee if the contract were upheld;

  ○ the hardship caused to the misrepresentor if the contract were rescinded. The Court of Appeal also stated that the damages should resemble damages for breach of warranty;

- it is not clear whether 'damages in lieu' can be awarded if one of the bars to recision apply;

- where the misrepresentation has become a term of the contract the misrepresentee can sue for damages for breach of contract, as an alternative to damages for misrepresentation.

Duress

A common law doctrine.

> Duress involves coercion.

Duress to the person

This requires actual or threatened violence to the person. Originally, it was the only form of duress recognised by the law.

Duress to goods

- Threat of damage to goods – traditionally this has not been recognised by the law; but in view of the development of economic duress, it is assumed that duress to goods would today be a ground for relief.

Economic duress

Economic duress led to rescission of a contract in *Universe Tankships of Monrovia v ITWF* (1983) where the union had 'blacked' a tanker, and refused to let it leave port until certain moneys had been paid. The House of Lords considered that this amounted to economic duress and ordered return of the money.

It has been stated that economic duress requires:

Compulsion or coercion of the will

In *Pau On v Lau Yiu Long* (1980) Lord Scarman listed the following indications of compulsion or coercion of the will.

- Did the party coerced have an alternative course open to him?

- Did the party coerced protest?

- Did the party coerced have independent advice?

- Did the party coerced take steps to avoid the contract?

Illegitimate pressure

There must be some element of illegitimacy in the pressure exerted, eg a threatened breach of contract. Economic duress is often pleaded together with lack of consideration in cases where a breach of contract is threatened by the promisor, unless he receives additional payment.

- In *Atlas Express v Kafco* (1989) Kafco, a small company which imported and distributed basketware, had a contract to supply Woolworths. They contracted with Atlas for delivery of the basketware to Woolworths. The contract commenced, then Atlas discovered they had under-priced the contract, and told Kafco that unless they paid a minimum sum for each consignment, they would cease to deliver. Kafco were heavily dependant on the Woolworth contract, and knew that a failure to deliver would lead both to the loss of the contract and an action for damages. At that time of the year, they could not find an alternative carrier, and agreed, under protest, to make the extra payments. Atlas sued for Kafko's non-payment. Held – the agreement was invalid for economic duress; and also for lack of consideration.

- *cf Williams v Roffey Bros* (1989) – Chapter 2.

The following threats are not illegitimate:

- a threat not to enter into a contract;

- a threat to institute civil proceedings;

- a threat to call the police.

- In *CTN Cash and Carry v Gallaher* (1994) it was confirmed that economic duress would not cover a legitimate threat, – in that case, a threat to withdraw credit facilities.

Note, not all threatened breaches of contract will amount to economic duress. It will only do so when the threatened party has no reasonable alternative open to him. The normal response to a breach of contract is to sue for damages.

Remedies

> Duress renders a contract voidable. Rescission will normally be sought from the courts. See above.

- In *North Ocean Shipping Co v Hyundai Construction Co, The Atlantic Baron* (1979) the court found economic duress but refused rescission on the ground that the plaintiff had affirmed the contract.

Undue influence

An equitable doctrine.

> Pressure not amounting to duress at common law, whereby a party is excluded from the exercise of free and independent judgment.

- Undue influence is based on the misuse of a relationship of trust or confidence between the parties. Where found, it renders a contract voidable. The innocent party will need to apply to the court for rescission of the contract (see above).

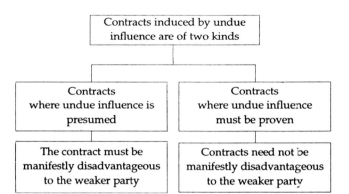

Contracts where undue influence is presumed

For example:

- Contracts between certain relationships:

  parent and child

  trustee and beneficiary

  solicitor and client

  doctor and patient

  religious adviser and disciple;

- Where there has been a long relationship of confidence and trust between the parties

  eg between husband and wife or where one party had been accustomed to rely for guidance and advice on the other. In *Lloyd's Bank v Bundy* (1975) Mr Bundy, an elderly west country farmer, on the advice of the local Lloyds Bank assistant manager, granted a charge to the bank over the family farm, to guarantee his son's indebtedness to the bank. Mr Bundy had, all his life, relied on Lloyds Bank for financial advice; the court set aside the charge on the ground of undue influence on the part of the bank.

Note, a bank does not incur undue influence in normal circumstances.

In *National Westminster Bank v Morgan* (1985) the court held that the normal commercial relationship of banker and customer had not been displaced.

The stronger party can disprove undue influence by showing that:

- full disclosure of all material facts was made;
- the consideration was adequate;
- the weaker party was in receipt of independent legal advice.

Contracts where undue influence has to be proved
The burden of proof lies on the plaintiff to show that such influence did exist and was exerted.

Effect of undue influence on a third party
In *Barclays Bank v O'Brien* (1993) Mrs O'Brien had signed a guarantee which used the jointly owned matrimonial home as security for a loan made to her husband's business. Her husband had told her it was for a maximum of £60,000, but in fact it was for £130,000. Mrs O'Brien had not been advised by the bank to consult an independent solicitor. The House of Lords held that there was no undue influence in this case, but there was misrepresentation on the part of the husband. They further held that where there was undue influence or misrepresentation or other legal wrong, then the injured party's right to have the transaction set aside would be

enforceable also against the third party, provided the third party had actual or constructive notice of the wrong. Such notice would arise where:

- the parties were in an emotional relationship, eg cohabitees (heterosexual or homosexual) or child and aged parents.

- one party was undertaking a financial liability on behalf of the other which was not to her or his advantage;

The court also held that in the above situation the third party could discharge his duty by making clear to the party concerned the full nature of the risk he or she is taking on, eg

- by conducting a personal interview, or

- urging independent advice;

Note, this doctrine of constructive notice applies to sureties (guarantors) but does not apply where a bank makes a joint loan to both parties as the facts in that situation do not meet the requirements set out in *Barclays Bank v O'Brien*. See *CIBC Mortgages v Pitt* (1993).

Note

- A failure by a solicitor to give proper advice, cannot be held against a bank.

- Once undue influence or misrepresentation has been found, the whole contract is avoided; it cannot be upheld in part.

- Damages are not available as a remedy for duress or undue influence.

6 Mistake

There is much disagreement concerning the effect of mistake on a contract. There are many reasons for this: confusion as to which terms to use; there are a large number of cases which can be interpreted in different ways; there are no recent decisive House of Lords decisions on the subject; the intervention of equity.

Terminology

Different terms are used by Cheshire and Anson to describe the same kind of mistake, and you should ascertain which terms are used in your textbook.

	CHESHIRE	**ANSON**	**Effect**
Same mistake made by both parties	Common mistake	Mutual mistake	May nullify agreement
Parties at cross-purposes	Mutual mistake	Unilateral mistake	Negatives agreement
Parties at cross-purposes, but one party knows that the other is mistaken	Unilateral mistake	Unilateral mistake	Negatives agreement

The terms used by Cheshire are used in these notes.

> In common mistakes,
> the parties are agreed but both are mistaken.

> In mutual and unilateral mistakes,
> the parties may not have reached agreement,
> and these mistakes are sometimes dealt with
> under the heading of agreement.

Effect of a mistake

> The general rule is that a mistake has no effect
> on a contract, but certain mistakes of a fundamental
> nature, sometimes called operative mistakes may
> render a contract void.

If the contract is rendered void, then the parties will be returned to their original positions, and this may defeat the rights of innocent third parties who may have acquired an interest in the contract.

The reluctance of the courts to develop the common law doctrine of mistake is probably due to the unfortunate consequences for third parties that can result from holding a contract void.

Operative mistakes

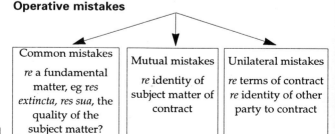

Common mistakes	Mutual mistakes	Unilateral mistakes
re a fundamental matter, eg *res extincta, res sua*, the quality of the subject matter?	*re* identity of subject matter of contract	*re* terms of contract *re* identity of other party to contract

Common mistakes

> The parties are agreed, but they are both under the same misapprehension. If this misapprehension is sufficiently fundamental it may nullify the agreement.

- At common law, this may render the contract void: ie the contract has no legal effect; it is unenforcable by either party and title to property cannot pass under it.

- At equity a more flexible approach has developed; contracts containing certain common mistakes have been treated as voidable. In setting aside such contracts the courts have a much wider control over the terms it can impose on the parties.

In *Bell v Lever Bros* (1932) it was stated that to nullify the agreement, the 'mistake must go to the root of the contract'. Lever Bros agreed to pay two directors of a subsidiary company substantial sums of money in compensation for loss of office, while unaware of the fact that they had engaged in irregular conduct which would have allowed them to be dismissed without pay. There was therefore a common mistake as to the validity of the contracts of employment. Lever Bros asked the court to order the return the compensation paid on the ground that it had been paid as a result of a common mistake. The House of Lords held that the common mistake concerning the validity of the contract of service was not 'sufficiently fundamental' to render the contract void.

Common mistakes 'sufficiently fundamental' to render a contract void

A common mistake as to the existence of the subject matter (res extincta)

- In *Galloway v Galloway* (1914) the parties, believing they were married, entered into a separation agreement. Later they discovered that they were not validly married. Held – the separation agreement was void for a common mistake

- In *Strickland v Turner* (1852) the court declared void on the grounds of a common mistake a contract to purchase an annuity on the life of a person who had already died.

- In *Couturier v Hastie* (1856) a buyer bought a cargo of corn which both parties believed to be at sea: the cargo had, however, already been disposed of. Held – the contract was void.

- Section 6 Sale of Goods Act 1979 declares that 'Where there is a contract for the sale of specific goods, and the goods without the knowledge of the seller have perished when the contract is made, the contract is void.

  However in *McRae v Commonwealth Disposals Commission* (1951) the commission sold to McRae the right to salvage a tanker lying on a specified reef. There was no such reef of that name, nor was there any tanker. The court found that there was a valid contract and that the commission had impliedly guaranteed the existence of the tanker. The case could be distinguished from the Australian equivalent of s 6 on the ground that there never had been a tanker and it had, therefore, not perished.

  Whether a contract is void, or valid depends on the construction of the contract, ie even if the subject matter does not exist, the contract will be valid:

- if performance was guaranteed; or

- if it was the purchase of a 'chance';

  otherwise, the contract would be void (*Anson* and others).

Mistake as to title – res sua ie the thing sold already belongs to the buyer

- In *Cooper v Phibbs* (1867) Cooper, not realising that a fishery already belonged to him, agreed to lease it from Phibbs. Held – the contract was void.

Mistake as to the possibility of performing the contract

- In *Sheik Bros Ltd v Ochsner* (1957) a contract was held void as the land was not capable of growing the crop contracted for.

- In *Griffith v Brymer* (1903) a contract to hire a room to view the coronation of Edward VII and which was made after the procession had been cancelled was held void. (Commercial impossibility.)

Mistake as to the quality of the subject matter

Lords Atkin and Thankerton both insisted in *Bell v Lever Bros* that to render a contract void, the mistake must go to the 'root of the contract'.

- It has been argued that if the mistake in *Bell* was not sufficiently fundamental to render a contract void, then it is highly unlikely that any mistake concerning quality would do so.

- Similarly, in *Leaf v International Galleries* (1950) where both parties mistakenly believed that a painting was by Constable, the Court of Appeal stated that the contract was not void for common mistake.

- In *Solle v Butcher* (1950) the Court of Appeal declined to declare void a lease which both parties believed was not subject to the Rent Acts. A similar decision was reached in *Grist v Bailey* (1967) where the parties both believed that a house was subject to a protected tenancy.

However Lord Justice Stein in *Associated Japanese Bank v Credit du Nord* (1988) stated that not enough attention had been paid to speeches in *Bell v Lever Bros* which did indicate that a narrow range of mistakes in quality could render a contract void, eg Lord Atkin's statement that 'A contract may be void if the mistake is as to the existence of some quality which makes the thing without that quality essentially different from the thing it was believed to be'. He gave as an example – if a horse believed to be sound turns out to be unsound then the contract remains valid; but if a a horse believed to be a racehorse, turns out to be a carthorse – then the contract is void.

Equity

> Lord Justice Stein in
> *Associated Japanese Bank v Credit du Nord* (1988)
> stated that a court will first examine whether a
> contract is void at common law; if it is not, then it
> will examine whether equity will grant rescission.

The role of equity according to this view is supplementary, designed to relieve the limitations of the common law.

- Rescission on terms was granted by the Court of Appeal in *Solle v Butcher* (1950) (see above). The court rescinded the lease, but gave the tenant the option of staying there on terms of his paying the extra rent which the landlord could have charged in view of the improvements.

- Rescission on terms was also granted in *Grist v Bailey* (1967) where a house was sold in the mistaken belief that it had a protected tenancy and in *Laurence v Lexcourt Holdings* (1978) where there was a common mistake with regard to planning permission.

- Rescission without terms was granted in *Magee v Pennine Insurance Co* (1969) where an agreement by an insurance company to meet a claim was rescinded because the parties were unaware that it was based on a policy which was voidable due to a misrepresentation by the assured.

It has been pointed out, however, that this decision is in direct conflict with the House of Lords decision in *Bell v Lever Bros* where a contract was held valid despite the parties failing to realise that it was based on a voidable contract of employment. Both cases turned on the mistaken belief that a contract was valid when in fact it was voidable.

The previous cases could have been distinguished from *Bell* on the ground that they all concerned property.

Mutual and unilateral mistakes

> These mistakes negate consent
> ie prevent the formation of an agreement.

The courts adopt an objective test in deciding whether agreement has been reached. It is not enough for one of the parties to allege that he was mistaken.

Mistake can negate consent in the following cases.

Mutual mistakes concerning the identity of the subject matter

> In these cases the parties are at cross-purposes, but there must have been some ambiguity in the situation before the courts will declare the contract void.

- In *Raffles v Wichelhaus* (1864) a consignment of cotton was bought to arrive 'ex *Peerless* from Bombay'. Two ships, both called *Peerless* were due to leave Bombay at around the same time. Held – no agreement as the buyer was thinking of one ship, and the seller was referring to the other ship.

- Similarly there was no agreement in *Scriven Bros v Hindley & Co Ltd* (1913) where the seller sold 'tow' and the buyer bought 'hemp'. Again there was an ambiguity as both lots were delivered under the same shipping mark and the catalogue was vague.

- But in *Smith v Hughes* (1871) the court refused to declare void an agreement whereby the buyer had thought he was buying old oats when in fact they were new oats, as the contract was for the sale of 'oats'. The mistake related to the quality not the identity of the subject matter.

Unilateral mistake concerning the terms of the contract

> Here one party has taken advantage of the other party's error.

- In *Hartog v Colin & Shields* (1939) the seller mistakenly offered to sell goods at a given price per pound when they intended to offer them per piece. All the preliminary negotiations had been on the basis of per piece. The buyers must have realised that the sellers had made a mistake. The contract was declared void.

- In *Smith v Hughes,* however, the contract was for the sale of 'oats' not 'old oats'; it would only have been void if 'old oats' had been a term of the contract.

Unilateral mistake as to the identity of other parties to the contract

There are a number of contradictory cases and theories under this heading.

Traditionally, a distinction is made between mistakes as to identity and mistakes as to attributes (eg credit worthiness). In *Cundy v Lindsay* (1878) a Mr Blenkarn ordered goods from Lindsay signing the letter to give the impression that the order came from Blenkiron & Co, a firm known to Lindsay & Co. Held – the contract was void. Lindsay & Co had only intended to do business with Blenkiron & Co. There was therefore a mistake concerning the identity of the other party to the contract.

- In *King's Norton Metal Co v Edridge Merrett & Co Ltd* (1872) on the other hand, a Mr Wallis ordered goods on impressive stationery which indicated that the order had come from Hallam & Co, an old established firm with branches all over the country. Held the contract between Kings Norton Metal Co and Wallis was not void. The sellers intended to do business with the writer of the letter, they were merely mistaken as to his attributes, ie the size and credit worthiness of his business.

- In *Boulton v Jones* (1857) the defendant sent an order for some goods to a Mr Brocklehurst unaware that he had sold the business to his foreman, the plaintiff. The plaintiff supplied the goods but the defendant refused to pay for them as he had only intended to do business with Brocklehurst against whom he had a set-off. Held, there was a mistake concerning the identity of the other party and the contract was therefore void.

> From the above three cases, it would seem that a contract is void if the mistaken party intended to do business with another specific person, and the identity of that other person was important to him.

However, the cases all concerned contracts negotiated at a distance.

> Where the parties are *inter praesentes*, the same rules apply, but there is a presumption that the innocent party intended to do business with the person physically in his presence.

- In *Phillips v Brooks* (1919) a jeweller sold a gold ring and delivered it on credit to a customer who had come into his shop and had falsely claimed to be Sir George Bullock, a well known and wealthy man. Held – the contract was valid, the jeweller had intended to do business with the person in his shop.

- In *Lewis v Averay* (1972) a rogue claimed to be Richard Green the film actor and produced a pass to Pinewood studios in the name of Richard Green to verify this. He was allowed to drive away a car in return for a cheque and subsequently resold the car for cash to Averay. The cheque bounced, and the seller claimed the return of the car on the ground that he was mistaken as to the identity of the buyer. Held – the contract was valid. The seller must be presumed to have intended to deal with the person physically in the room with him. Averay kept the car.

There are two cases, however, where the plaintiffs were able to establish a mistake as to the identity of a person in their presence.

- In *Ingram v Little* (1961) two sisters sold a car and handed it over against a worthless cheque to a person who claimed to be a Mr Hutchinson of Stanstead House, Caterham. They only did so after one of them had checked that there was a man of that name who lived at that address. The Court of Appeal held the contract void. They considered that the sisters had done enough to establish that they only intended to deal with Mr Hutchinson.

This case has been greatly criticised as it is difficult to reconcile with *Phillips v Brooks* and *Lewis v Averay*.

- In *Sowler v Potter* (1940) the lease of a cafe was granted to Potter who had previously been convicted of keeping a disorderly cafe under the name of Robinson. The court held that the contract was void because of the lessor's mistaken belief that Potter was not Robinson. This case has also been much criticised and doubted, as it did not seem that Sowler had intended to do business with any other identifiable person. The contract could, in any case, have been set aside for misrepresentation.

The contract would in most cases be voidable in any case for misrepresentation where one party has misled the other with regard to his identity. The advantage of having the contract declared void for mistake is to avoid the bars to rescission.

See Chapter 6.

Mistake as to the nature of the document signed

Defence of *non est factum*.

• The scope of this defence has been limited since the decision in *Saunders v Anglia Building Society* (*Gallie v Lee*) (1971) where an old lady was persuaded by her nephew to sign a document conveying her house to her nephew's friend. She had believed that she was singing a deed of gift to her nephew. She had not read the document because her glasses were broken. It was held that the document was valid. It was stated that:

The signed document must be fundamentally different in effect from what it was thought to be.
The signatory must prove that he had not been negligent in signing the document.

It is also thought that it will only protect a person who is under some disability. The defence did succeed in *Lloyd's Bank v Waterhouse* (1990) where the defendant who was illiterate signed a guarantee of his son's debt to the bank. The father thought that the guarantee covered the purchase price of a farm but in fact it covered all his son's indebtedness to the bank. It was held that the effect of the document was fundamentally different from what it was believed to be, there was no negligence and the contract was therefore void.

In *UDT Ltd v Western* (1976) it was held that these same rules applied to cases where a person had signed a form before all the details required by the form had been entered.

Mistake in equity

The narrow approach taken by the common law towards mistake is supplemented by the more flexible approach of equity. The following remedies may be available.

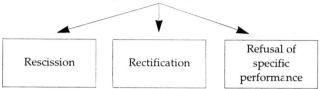

| Rescission | Rectification | Refusal of specific performance |

Rescission
See common mistake (above).

Rectification
Where there has been a mistake, not in the actual agreement but in reducing it to writing, equity will order rectification of the document so that it coincides with the true agreement of the parties.

Necessary conditions
- The document does not represent the intention of both parties.

- If one party mistakenly believed a term was included in the document, and the other party knew of this error. In *Roberts & Co Ltd v Leicestershire CC* (1961) the completion date of a contract was rectified at the request of one party because it was clear that the other party was aware of the error when the contract was signed.

  If the document fails to mention a term which one party but not the other had intended to be a term of the contract, there is no case for rectification.

- There must have been a concluded agreement, but not necessarily a legally enforceable contract. In *Joscelyne v Nissen* (1970) a father and daughter agreed that the daughter should take over the car-hire business. In return the father would continue to live in the house and the daughter would pay all the household expenses. This last provision was not included in the written contract. Held – the contract should be rectified to include it.

Note, a document which accurately records a prior agreement cannot be rectified because the agreement was made under some mistake (*Rose v Pym*, above). Equity rectifies documents not agreements.

Rectification is an equitable remedy and is available at the discretion of the court. Lapse of time or third party rights may prevent rectification.

Refusal of specific performance

> Specific performance will be refused when the contract is void at common law. Equity may also refuse specific performance where a contract is valid at law, but only 'where a hardship amounting to injustice would have been inflicted upon him by holding him to his bargain'.

- In *Webster v Cecil* (1861) the defendant having previously refused the plaintiff's offer of £2,000 for his land, wrote to the plaintiff offering to sell it to him for £1,250 instead of £2,250 as he had intended. The plaintiff accepted the offer. Specific performance was refused as the plaintiff must have been aware of the error (unilateral mistake).

- Where there is no blame on the plaintiff the situation is more difficult. In *Malins v Freeman* (1837) the defendant had mistakenly bought the wrong property at an auction. Specific performance was refused. In *Tamplin v James* (1879) however, the court ordered specific performance where the defendant had bid for a property under an error as to its true extent. Presumably being forced to buy a totally different property from the one he intended would have caused greater hardship than being forced to buy a property whose dimensions differed from his expectations.

7 Illegality and capacity

Illegal contracts are classified in different ways by different authorities. In this chapter, the classification used by Cheshire, Fifoot and Furmston is followed.

Illegality

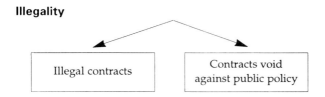

| Illegal contracts | Contracts void against public policy |

The main issue with regard to illegal contracts is the effect of illegality on a contract. The most often examined topic with regard to contracts which are declared void on grounds of public policy are contracts in restraint of trade.

Illegal contracts

Contracts illegal by statute

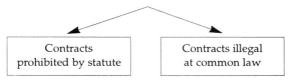

| Contracts prohibited by statute | Contracts illegal at common law |

- Statute may declare a contract illegal, eg The Restrictive Trade Practices Act 1976.

- Statute may prohibit an act, but declare that it shall not effect validity of contract, eg The Trade Descriptions Act 1968.

- Statute may prohibit an act but not stipulate its effect on the contract. The status of the contract will in this case be a matter of interpretation for the court. In *Re Mahmoud & Ispahani* (1921) the court decided that a statement that 'a person shall not buy or otherwise deal in linseed oil without a license' was a prohibition, and a contract entered into by a person without a license was therefore void.

- The courts are reluctant to imply a prohibition when this is not clearly indicated in the statute. In *Hughes v Asset Managers* (1995) the court held a contract valid despite the fact that a document had not been signed by a person authorised to do so as required by statute.

Contracts illegal at common law

- An agreement to commit a crime, a tort or a fraud, eg defraud the rating authority (*Allen v Roscous* (1676)); to publish a libel (*Clay v Yates*).

- An agreement to defraud the Inland Revenue (*Napier v Business Associates* (1951)).

- Contracts damaging to the country's safety or foreign relations.

- Contracts interfering with the course of justice, eg contracts to give false evidence.

- Contracts leading to corruption in public life (*Parkinson v Royal College of Ambulance* (1925)).

- Contracts tending to promote sexual immorality (*Pearce v Brooks* (1866)).

Effects of illegality

```
                    ┌──────────────┴──────────────┐
┌──────────────────────────┐      ┌──────────────────────────┐
│    Contracts illegal      │      │    Contracts illegal      │
│       as formed           │      │   in their performance    │
└──────────────────────────┘      └──────────────────────────┘
```

Contracts illegal as formed

> Such contracts are void *ab initio*:
> there can be no action for breach of contract.

In *Pearce v Brooks* (1866) the owner of a coach of unusual design, was unable to recover the cost of hire from a prostitute who, to his knowledge, had hired it in order to attract clients (unjust enrichment?).

> Money paid, or property transferred under
> the contract cannot be recovered.

In *Parkinson v Royal College of Ambulance* (1925) Parkinson was unable to recover the money he had donated to the defendants on the understanding that they would obtain a knighthood for him.

Exceptions
- Where the parties are not *in pari delicto*, eg where one party is unaware of the illegal nature of the contract, or has been induced to enter into it by fraudulent misrepresentation, or is the party the law was attempting to protect, eg a tenant who had paid an illegal premium could recover it (*Kiriri Cotton Co v Dewani* (1960)).

- Where the transferor genuinely repents and repudiates the contract before performance. In *Tribe v Tribe* (1995) money was transferred to a son in order to avoid the father's creditors. At the end of the day the creditors were all paid in full, and the father was allowed to cite the original reason for the transfer in order to repudiate the presumption of advancement. He had withdrawn from the illegal purpose before performance.

In *Bigos v Boustead* (1951) however, the court was not convinced that the plaintiff had genuinely repented.

- Where the transferor can frame his claim without relying on the contract. In *Bowmakers v Barnet Instruments* (1945) the plaintiffs delivered and were able to rely on an action in the tort of conversion to recover goods held under an illegal hire-purchase contract.

Similarly, in *Tinsley v Milligan* (1993) both parties had contributed money towards the purchase of a house put in the name of Tinsley alone in order to allow Milligan to make various social security claims. When Milligan sued for the return of the money, it was argued that the agreement had been entered into for an illegal purpose and that the public conscience 'would be affronted by recognising rights created by illegal transactions'. The House of Lords held, however, that a resulting trust had been created in favour of Milligan by the contribution to the purchase price. Milligan, therefore could rely on the resulting trust and had no need to rely on the illegal agreement.

This case shows (a) that the rule applies to equity as well as to common law, (b) the test of 'affront to the public conscience' developed by the Court of Appeal, and applied to this case by the Court of Appeal is not good law.

- Collateral contracts are tainted with the illegality and are void, eg a promissory note issued in connection with the contract.

- Where part of the contract is lawful, the court will not sever the good from the bad. In *Napier v National Business Agency* (1951) certain payments were described as 'expenses' in order to defraud the Inland Revenue. The court refused to enforce payment of the accompanying salary, as the whole contract was tainted with the illegality.

Note property can pass under an illegal contract, as in *Sing v Ali* (1960).

Contracts illegal in their performance

> The illegality may only arise during the performance of a contract, eg a carrier may break the law by exceeding the speed limit whilst delivering goods belonging to a client. He will be punished, but the contract will not necessarily be void.

A claim by the innocent party to enforce the contract in these cases is strong.

- In *Marles v Philip Trant* (1954) the defendant sold winter wheat described as spring wheat, without an accompanying invoice as required by statute. Held – the plaintiff could sue for damages for breach of contract. The contract was illegal in its performance, but not in its inception.

- In *Strongman v Simcock* (1955) Simcock failed to get licences which were needed to modernise some houses which belonged to him, and refused to pay for the work on the basis that the contracts were illegal. Held – Strongman could not sue on the illegal contracts, but could sue Simcock on his collateral promise to obtain the licenses.

- In *Archbolds v Spanglett* (1961) Spanglett contracted to carry Archbolds whisky in a van which was not licensed to carry any goods other than his own. Archbold was unaware of this and could therefore recover damages for breach of contract.

  But, in *Ashmore, Benson, Pease, & Co v Dawson Ltd* (1973), the other party knew of the overloading of the lorry, and could not therefore recover damages. He had, therefore, participated in the illegality.

- Even the guilty party may enforce the contract, if the illegality is incidental.

  In *Shaw v Groom* (1970) a landlord failed to give his tenant a rent book as required by law. Held – he could sue for the rent. The purpose of the statute was to punish the landlord's failure to provide a rent book not to render the contract void.

  In *St John Shipping v Rank* (1957) a ship owner who had overloaded his ship in contravention of a statute was able to recover freight.

Contracts void at common law on grounds of public policy

Contracts damaging to the institution of marriage.	Contracts to oust the jurisdiction of the courts.
eg contracts in restraint of marriage, marriage, brokerage contracts, contracts for future separation (pre-nuptial agreements).	However, arbitration agreements are valid.
Contracts made after or immediately before separation are valid.	

Contracts in restraint of trade

A contract in restraint of trade is *prima facie* void, but the courts will now uphold the restriction if it is shown that:

- the restraint is reasonable between the parties;

- the restraint is reasonable as regards the interest of the public.

In *Esso Petroleum v Harpers Garage* (1968) it was stated that the court will consider:

- whether the contract is in restraint of trade. A contract is in restraint of trade if it restricts a person's liberty to carry on his trade or profession. Certain restraints have become acceptable over the years, eg 'tied houses', restrictive covenants in leases, sole agency, or sole distributorship agreements;

- whether it should nevertheless be enforced because it is reasonable. The onus of proving reasonability is on the promisee. A restraint to be permissible must be no wider than is necessary to protect the relevant interest of the promisee.

Categories of contracts in restraint of trade

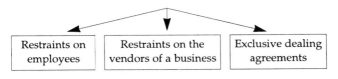

| Restraints on employees | Restraints on the vendors of a business | Exclusive dealing agreements |

Restraints on employees

The restraint is void, unless the employer can show:

- It is necessary to protect a proprietory interest
  ie the trade secrets of a works manager in *Foster v Suggett*
  (1918): the trade connections of a solicitor's managing
  clerk in *Fitch v Dewes* (1921).

- A restraint merely to prevent competition will not be
  enforced.

  In *Eastham v Newcastle United FC* (1964) the court accepted that the proper organisation of football was a
  valid matter for clubs to protect, but found the 'retain
  and transfer system' unreasonable.

- The restraint is no greater than is necessary to protect
  the employer's interest in terms of time and area.

  In *Scorer v Seymore-Jones* (1966) the court upheld a
  restriction of 10 miles within branch A at which the
  employee had worked, but held that a similar restraint
  covering branch B at which the employee had not
  worked was unreasonable and void.

- Problems with area can be overcome by using 'non-
  solicitation' clauses instead.

  In *Home Counties Dairies v Skilton* (1970) a milkman
  agreed that for one year after leaving his present job, he
  would not sell milk to his employer's customers. Held –
  restraint valid. It was necessary to protect the employer
  against loss of customers.

- The validity of the duration of the restraint depends on
  the nature of the business to be protected, and on the
  status of the employee.

In *Briggs v Oates* (1991) a restriction of five miles for five years on an assistant solicitor was upheld as reasonable.

- A restraint imposed by indirect means, eg by loss of pension rights (*Bull v Pitney Bowes* (1966) or where two companies agreed not to take on each others employees (*Kores v Kolok*) will be judged by the same criteria.

Restraints on the vendor of a business

> Such a restraint is valid if it is intended to protect the purchasers interest in the goodwill of the business bought.

- In *Vancouver Malt and Sake Brewing Co v Vancouver Breweries Ltd* (1934) a company which was licensed to brew beer, but which had not at any time brewed beer, was sold, and agreed not to brew any beer for 15 years. Held – the restraint was void since there was no goodwill of a beer brewing business to be transferred.

- In *British Concrete v Schelff* (1921) S sold his localised business to B who had branches all over the UK and agreed not to open any business within 10 miles of any of B's branches. Held – the restriction was void. B was entitled only to protect the business he had bought not the business which he already owned.

- In *Nordenfelt v Maxim Nordenfelt* (1894) N, a world-wide supplier of guns, sold his world-wide business to M, and agreed not to manufacture guns anywhere in the world for 25 years. Held – the restriction was valid.

Exclusive dealing agreements

> *Solus* agreements, whereby A agrees to buy all his
> requirements of a particular commodity from B.

- In *Esso Petroleum v Harpers Garage* (1968) a *solus* agreement for four years was held reasonable, but a *solus*
  agreement for 21 years was held unreasonable, and
  therefore void.

- *Solus* agreements were distinguished from restrictive
  covenants in a lease. When an oil company leases a fill-
  ing station to X, inserting a clause that X should buy all
  its requirements from the company, this is not subject to
  restraint of trade rules because the tenant is not giving
  up a previously held freedom.

- But in *Amoco v Rocca Bros* (1975) the court held that
  restraint of trade rules did apply to lease and lease back
  agreements.

- In *Alec Lobb (Garages) v Total Oil* (1985) in a similar lease-
  back arrangement, a *solus* agreement for between 7 and
  21 years was held reasonable on the ground that the
  arrangement was a rescue operation benefiting the
  plaintiffs, and there were 'break' clauses in the under-
  lease.

> Most exclusive services contracts are found in
> professional sport or entertainment.

- In *Schroeder Music Publishing Co v Macaulay* (1974) it was
  held that a contract by which an unknown song writer
  undertook to give his exclusive services to a publisher
  who made no promise to publish his work was subject

to the restraint of trade doctrine, as it was 'capable of enforcement in an oppressive manner'.

- In *Greig v Insole* (1978) the MCC banned any cricketer who played for a cricketing 'circus' from playing for England. The court held that the ban was void as being in restraint of trade.

It has been suggested that the courts will hold exclusive dealing and service contracts to be within the restraint of trade doctrine, if they contain unusual or novel features, or if there is disparity in the bargaining power, and the agreement is likely to cause hardship to the weaker party.

Cartel agreements
These are now covered by statute, eg The Fair Trading Act 1973, The Resale Prices Act 1976, The Restrictive Trade Practices Act 1976, The Competition Act 1980, and The Treaty of Rome.

Effect of a restraint

A void restraint is severable. Severance can be operated in two ways:

- severance of the whole of the objectionable promise, leaving the rest of the contract to be enforced;

- severance of the objectionable part of the promise.

Two tests must be satisfied:

○ The 'blue pencil' test. It must be possible to sever the illegal part simply by deleting words in the contract. The court will not add words, substitute one word for another, or rearrange words or in any way redraft the contract. In *Mason v Provident Clothing Co Ltd*

(1913), the House of Lords refused to redraft a promise not to work within 25 miles of London. But in *Goldsoll v Goldman* (1915) a dealer in imitation jewellery promised not to deal in real or imitation jewellery either in the UK or abroad. Dealing in real jewellery and dealing abroad was severed.

○ Severance of the objectionable part of the contract must not alter the nature (as distinct from the extent) of the original contract; the illegal restraint will not be severed if it is the the main purpose of the restraint, or if to sever it would alter entirely the scope and intention of the agreement. In *Attwood v Lamont* (1920) the court refused to sever restrictions on a tailor from competing with any department of the department store which had employed him. The court stated that this was a covenant 'which must stand or fall in its unaltered form'.

Capacity

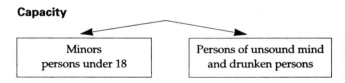

| Minors
persons under 18 | Persons of unsound mind
and drunken persons |

Minors

The law pursues two conflicting policies in the case of minors. On the one hand it tries to protect minors from their own inexperience; on the other, it tries to ensure that persons dealing with minors are not dealt with in a harsh manner.

Contracts with minors can be divided into three categories.

| Valid contracts | Voidable contracts | Other contracts |

Valid contracts – contracts which can be enforced against a minor

Contracts for necessaries	Beneficial contracts of service

Necessaries

> Necessary goods are defined in the Sale of Goods Act 1979 as 'goods suitable to his condition in life, and to his actual requirements at the time of sale and delivery'.

- In *Nash v Inman* (1908) a student purchased 11 silk waistcoats while still a minor. The court held that silk waistcoats were suitable to the conditions of life of a Cambridge undergraduate at that time, but they were not suitable to his actual needs as he already had a sufficient supply of waistcoats.

It is important to distinguish between luxurious goods of utility, and goods of pure luxury. The status of the minor can make the former into necessaries, but the latter can never be classified as necessaries.

The burden of proving that the goods are necessaries are on the seller.

> Necessary services include education, medical and legal services.

They must satisfy the same tests as necessary goods.

Professor Treitel considers that both executed and unexecuted contracts for necessaries can be enforced. He cites *Roberts*

v Gray (1913). Roberts agreed to take Grey, a minor, on a billiard tour to instruct him in the profession of billiard player. Grey repudiated the contract. The court held that Roberts could recover damages despite the fact that the contract was executory.

Cheshire, Fifoot and Furmston agree that executory contracts for necessary services are enforceable as in *Roberts v Gray* but deny that executory contracts for necessary goods can be enforced.

They cite:

- The actual wording of the SGA which refers to time of 'sale and delivery'.

- the minor has to pay a reasonable price for the goods not the contractual price.

These indicate, it is argued, that liability is based on acceptance of the goods not on agreement.

Beneficial contracts of service

> These must be for the benefit of the minor.

- In *De Francesco v Barnum* (1890) a contract whose terms were burdensome and harsh on the minor, was held void.

- But in *White City Stadium v Doyle* (1935) where a minor had forfeited his payment for a fight because of disqualification, the contract was nevertheless enforceable against him. Where a contract is on the whole for the benefit of a minor, it will not be invalidated because one term has operated in a way which is not to his advantage.

> They must be contracts of service
> or similar to a contract of service.

- In *Chaplin v Leslie Frewin (Publishers) Ltd* (1966) the court enforced a contract by a minor to publish his memoirs as this would train him in becoming an author, and enable him to earn a living.

- But trading contracts (involving the minor's capital) will not be enforced even if it does help the minor earn a living. In *Mercantile Union Guarantee Co Ltd v Ball* (1937) the court refused to enforce a hire purchase contract for a lorry which would enable a minor to trade as a haulage contractor.

Voidable contracts

> Contracts which can be avoided by the minor before majority or within a short time afterwards.

These comprise contracts of continuing obligation such as contracts to acquire an interest in land, or partly paid shares, or partnership agreements.

The minor can free himself from obligations for the future, eg an obligation to pay rent under a lease, but will have to pay for benefits already received. He cannot recover money already paid under the contract unless there has been a total failure of consideration (*Steinberg v Scala (Leeds) Ltd* (1923)).

Other contracts

> These cannot be enforced against a minor.

But:

- The minor himself may enforce such contracts.

- Property can pass under such contracts.

- Where the contract has been carried out by the minor, he cannot recover any property unless there has been a total failure of consideration, or some other failing which would equally apply to an adult.

- The Minors Contracts Act 1987 provides that:

  ○ a minor may ratify such a contract on majority, and it can thereafter be enforced against him;

  ○ a guarantee of a minor's debt will not be void because a minor's debt is unenforceable against him;

  ○ a court may, if it considers it is just and equitable to do so, order a minor to return property he has received under a void contract or any property representing it. It is not clear whether property transferred under the contract covers money, eg in money lending contracts. It is argued that as 'property representing it' must cover money, it would therefore be illogical to exclude money acquired directly, but there is as yet no decision on this point. Property cannot presumably be recovered under this section where the minor has given away the contract property.

- Equity will order restitution of property acquired by fraud. But there can be no restitution of money (*Leslie v Sheill* (1914)) and no restitution if the minor has resold the property.

- An action may be brought in tort if it does not in any way rely on the contract. But although a minor is fully liable for all his torts, he may not be sued in tort if this is just an indirect way of enforcing a contract. In *Leslie v Sheill* (1914) a minor obtained a loan by fraudulently misrepresenting his age. Held – he could not be sued in the tort of deceit as this would be an indirect way of enforcing a contract which was void.

Persons of unsound mind and drunken persons

A person who has been declared a 'patient' under the Mental Health Act 1983 by the Court of Protection is incapable of entering in to a valid contract.

Other mentally disordered persons and drunken persons will be bound by their contracts unless:

- they were so disordered or drunk that they did not understand the nature of what they were doing; and

- the other party was aware of this.

Such contracts may be affirmed during a sober or lucid moment. The Sale of Goods Act requires that where 'necessaries are sold and delivered to a person who by reason of mental incapacity or drunkenness is incompetent to contract, he must pay a reasonable price for them'.

8 Discharge

> There are no obligations outstanding
> under the contract

A contract may be discharged by

| Performance | Agreement | Breach | Frustration |

Performance

| Precision of performance | Time of performance | Tender of performance |

Precision of performance

> To discharge his obligations under a contract, a
> party must perform exactly what he promised.

- In *Cutter v Powell* (1795) a ship's engineer undertook to
  sail a ship from Jamaica to Liverpool, but died before the
  voyage was complete. Held – nothing could be recovered in respect of his service; he had not fulfilled his obligation.

- In *Bolton v Mahadeva* (1972) a central heating system gave
  out less heat than it should, and there were fumes in one
  room. Held, the contractor could not claim payment;
  although the boiler and pipes had been installed, they
  did not fulfill the primary purpose of heating the house.

These are examples of 'entire' contracts, which consists of one unseverable obligation. See also *Sumpter v Hedges* (1898).

> Despite the rule that performance must be exact, the law will allow payment to be made, on a *quantum meruit* basis, for incomplete performance in the following circumstances.

- Where the contract is divisible, payment can be recovered for the completed part, eg goods delivered by instalments.

- Where the promisee accepts partial performance. In *Sumpter v Hedges* (1898) however, payment for partial performance was refused as Hedges had been left with a half-built house, and had been put in a position where he had no choice but to accept partial performance.

- Where the promisee prevents complete performance, eg in *Planché v Colburn* (1831) a writer was allowed payment for the work he had already done when the publisher abandoned the series.

- Where the promisor has performed a substantial part of the contract. In *Hoenig v Isaacs* (1952) the plaintiff decorated the defendants flat, but because of faulty workmanship the defendant had to pay £50 to another firm to finish the job. Held – the plaintiff was entitled to £150 (the contract price) minus the £50 paid to the other firm, *cf Bolton v Mahadeva* (1972) where the court declined to find substantial performance.

This has become known as the doctrine of substantial performance. In order to rely on this doctrine the plaintiff's failure to perform must amount only to a breach of warranty or a non-fundamental breach of an innominate term. It will not apply to a fundamental breach or to a breach of condition.

Time of performance

> Equity considers that time is not
> 'of the essence of a contract', ie a condition,
> except in the following circumstances.

- It is stipulated in the contract, see *Lombard North Central v Butterworth* (1987) (see Chapter 4).

- One party has given reasonable notice during the currency of the contract that performance must take place within a certain time. In *Rickards v Oppenheim* (1950) a car body which had been ordered from the plaintiffs was late. The defendants gave final notice to the plaintiff that unless it was delivered within three months they would cancel the order. Held – time had been made of the essence; the defendants could cancel the order.

- The nature of the contract makes it imperative that stipulations as to time should be observed, eg contracts for the sale of perishable goods.

    The LPA 1925 stipulated that terms as to the time of performance should be interpreted in the same way at common law as in equity. In *Rainieri v Miles* (1981) the House of Lords held that that meant that late performance would not give rise to a right to terminate, but would give rise to damages.

Tender of performance

If one party tenders performance which is refused, he may sue for breach of contract.

If payment is tendered and rejected, the obligation to **tender** payment is discharged, but the obligation to **pay** remains.

Agreement

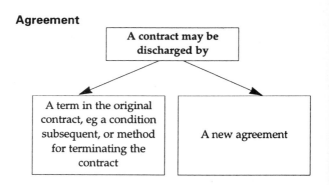

A contract may be discharged by

→ A term in the original contract, eg a condition subsequent, or method for terminating the contract

→ A new agreement

As contracts are created by agreement, so they may be discharged by agreement. Consideration is necessary to make the agreement binding.

- If the contract is wholly executory there is no problem with consideration as both parties surrender their rights under the contract.

- If the contract is partly executed – one party has completed his performance under the contract. To make the agreement binding there must either be a deed (a 'release') or new consideration ('accord and satisfaction') or the doctrine of equitable estoppel or waiver must apply. See Chapter 2.

Breach

A breach does not of itself discharge a contract. It may allow the other other party an option to treat the contract as discharged, ie to terminate the contract, if the breach is sufficiently serious,

ie if it is

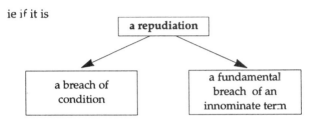

See classification of terms, Chapter 3.

There are special problems where a party repudiates a contract under a wrong assumption that he has a right to do so.

- In *Federal Commerce and Navigation v Molena Alpha* (1979) the owners of a ship gave instructions not to issue bills of lading without which the charterers could not operate the ship. They wrongly believed that they had the right to do so. Held – their conduct constituted a wrongful repudiation of the contract which allowed the other party to treat the contract as discharged.

- In *Woodar Investment Development v Wimpey Construction* (1980) the purchaser wrongly repudiated a contract for the sale land, wrongly believing that he had a right to do so. Held – not a wrongful repudiation which allowed the other party to treat the contract as discharged.

Cheshire, Fifoot and Furmston have distinguished the two decisions on the basis that there was no urgency in *Woodar*, the time for completion was some way off, and the seller could have sued for breach of contract. In *Molena Alpha*, on the other hand, the time before performance was very short putting much greater pressure on the charterers.

Effect of treating the contract as discharged

The obligation of both parties to perform (ie the primary obligation) is discharged from the date of the termination.

However, the party in breach may have to pay damages for any losses, past and future caused to the innocent party as a result of the breach (*Lombard North Central v Butterworth* – Chapter 3).

The discharge does not operate retrospectively. In *Photo Production v Securicor* (1980) Securicor was able to rely on an exclusion clause in the contract.

Note it was held by the Court of Appeal in *Vitol v Norelf* (1996) that the defendant's failure to perform his own obligation did not constitute acceptance of the plaintiff's repudiation.

The decision to terminate cannot be retracted.

Anticipatory breach of contract

Explicit	Implicit
Hochter v La Tour (1853) a travel courier announced in advance that he would not be fulfilling his contract.	*Frost v Knight* (1872) a party disabled himself from carrying out a promise to marry by marrying another person.

Effect

- The other party may sue for damages immediately. He does not have to await the date of performance (*Hochster v De La Tour* (1853)).

- The innocent party may refuse to accept the repudiation. He may affirm the contract and continue to perform his obligations under the contract. In *White and Carter Ltd v McGregor* (1962) the defendants cancelled a contract shortly after it had been signed. The plaintiffs refused to accept the cancellation, carried on with the contract, and then sued for the full contract price. Held – the plaintiffs were entitled to succeed; a repudiation does not automatically bring a contract to an end; the innocent party has an option either to affirm the contract or to terminate the contract, unless

  ○ the innocent party needs the cooperation of the other party. In *Hounslow BC v Twickenham Garden Developments Ltd* (1971) Hounslow council cancelled a contract to lay out a park. It was held that the defendants could not rely on *White and Carter v McGregor* because the work was to be performed on council property;

  ○ the innocent party had no legitimate interest, financial or otherwise in performing the contract, rather than in claiming damages. In *The Alaskan Trader* (1984) a ship chartered to the defendants required extensive repairs at the end of the first year, whereupon the defendants repudiated the contract. The plaintiffs, however, refused to accept the repudiation, repaired the ship, and kept it fully crewed ready for the defendant's use. Held – the plaintiffs had no special interest in keeping the contract alive. They should have accepted the repudiation and sued for damages.

Where a party has affirmed the contract

- He will have to pay damages for any subsequent breach by himself; he cannot argue that the other party's anticipatory breach excuses him (*Fercometal SARL v Mediterranean Shipping Co* (1988)).

- There is a danger that a supervening event may frustrate the contract and deprive the innocent party of his right to damages, as in *Avery v Bowden* (1855) (below).

Frustration

> Frustration occurs where it is established that due to a subsequent change in circumstances, the contract has become impossible to perform, or it has been deprived of its commercial purpose.

The doctrine has been kept to narrow limits

By the courts who have insisted that the supervening event must destroy a fundamental assumption.	By business persons who have 'drafted out' the doctrine by *force majeure* clauses.

The basis of the doctrine and the tests

- Until the 19th century, the courts adhered to a theory of 'absolute contracts', as in *Paradine v Jane* (1647). It was said that if the parties wished to evade liability because of some supervening event, then they should provide for this in the contract. However, in *Taylor v Caldwell* (1863) the courts relented, and held that if the contract became impossible to perform due to some extraneous cause for which neither party was responsible, then the contact would be discharged.

- The modern test was enunciated by Lord Simon in *National Carriers v Panalpina* (1981), 'supervenes an event which significantly changes the nature of the outstanding contractual rights ... that it would be unjust to hold the parties to them'.

- In *Davis Contractors v Fareham UDC* (1956), Lord Radcliff stated: 'Frustration occurs where to require performance would be to require something radically different from what was undertaken'.

> Note it is not the circumstances, but the nature of the obligation, which must have changed.

Circumstances in which frustration may occur

- The subject matter of the contract has been destroyed, or is otherwise unavailable.

  In *Taylor v Caldwell* (1863) a contract to hire a music hall was held to be frustrated by the destruction of the music hall by fire (see also s 7 SGA 1979).

- But the unavailable or destroyed object must have been intended by both parties to be the subject of the contract.

In *Blackburn Bobbin Co v Allen* (1918) the contract was for the sale of 'birch timber' which the seller intended to obtain from Finland. Held – the contract was not frustrated when it became impossible to obtain timber from Finland. The subject matter of the contract was birch timber not Finnish birch timber.

- Death or incapacity of a party to a contract of personal service, or a contract where the personality of one party is important.

In *Condor v The Baron Knights* (1966) a contract between a pop group and its drummer was held frustrated when the drummer became ill and was unable to fulfill the terms of the contract. A claim for unfair dismissal can also sometimes be defeated by the defence of frustration where an employee has become permanently incapacitated or imprisoned for a long period.

The contract has become illegal to perform, either because of a change in the law, or the outbreak of war.

In *Avery v Bowden* (1855) a contract to supply goods to Russia was frustrated when the Crimean War broke out on the ground that it had become an illegal contract – trading with the enemy.

Note the outbreak of war between two foreign states however, will not render a contract illegal, but may make it impossible to perform. In *Finelvet v Vinava Shipping Co* (1983) a contract to deliver goods to Basra, did not become illegal on the outbreak of the Iraq-Iran war, but was frustrated when it became too dangerous to sail to Basra.

- The commercial purpose of the contract has failed.

Establishing whether a contract is impossible or illegal to perform is relatively straight forward, but it is more difficult to decide whether the commercial purpose of the contract has failed.

It may happen in the following circumstances.

○ Failure of an event upon which the contract was based.

In *Krell v Henry* (1903), the court held that a contract to hire a room overlooking the proposed route of the coronation procession was frustrated when the coronation was postponed. The purpose of the contract was to view the coronation, not merely to hire a room. It has been argued that the fact that the hire of the room was a 'one-off' transaction was important. The judge in the case contrasted it with the hire of a taxi to take the client to Epsom on Derby day. This would be a normal contractual transaction for the taxi driver; the cancellation of the Derby would not therefore, frustrate the contract.

In the case of *Herne Bay Steamboat Co v Hutton* (1903) the court refused to hold frustrated a contract to hire a boat to see the king review the fleet when the review was cancelled; the fleet was still there and could be viewed – there was therefore no complete failure of the purpose of the contract.

○ Government interference or delay. In *Metropolitan Water Board v Dick Kerr* (1918) a contract had been formed in 1913 to build a reservoir within six years. In 1915, the government ordered the work to be stopped and the plant sold. Held – the contract was frustrated.

In *Jackson v Union Marine Insurance Co* (1874) a ship was chartered in November to proceed with all dispatch to Newport. The ship did not reach Newport until the following August. Held – the contract was frustrated since the ship was not available for the voyage for which she had been chartered.

In *The Nema* (1982) a charter party was frustrated when a long strike closed the port at which the ship was due to load, so that of the six or seven voyages contracted to be made between April and December, only two could be made.

Similar difficult problems arise in the case of contracts of employment (illness or imprisonment) and leases.

It has been suggested that where the contract is of a fixed duration, and the unavailability of the subject matter is only temporary, the court should consider the ratio of the likely interruption to the duration of the contract.

Leases

It had long been thought that the doctrine of frustration did not apply to leases (see *Paradine v Jane* (1647) and *Cricklewood Investments v Leighton's Investments* (1945)).

- However in *National Carriers v Panalpina* (1981) the House of Lords declared that in principle, a lease could be frustrated. In that case a street which gave the only access to a warehouse was closed for 18 months. The lease for the warehouse was for 10 years. Held – the lease was not frustrated.

- The House of Lords did state, however, that where there was only one purpose for the land/property leased, and this purpose became impossible, then the lease would be frustrated, eg a short term holiday lease (changed from never to hardly ever).

Limits to the doctrine of frustration

> 'Doctrine must be kept within narrow limits'.

It will not be applied:

> on the grounds of inconvenience,
> increase in expense, loss of profit.

- In *Davis Contractors LTD v Fareham UDC* (1956) the contractors had agreed to build a council estate at a fixed price. Due to strikes, bad weather, shortages of labour and materials, there were considerable delays and the houses could only be built at a substantial loss. Held – the contract was not frustrated.

- See also the *Suez* cases where the courts refused to hold shipping contracts frustrated as a result of the closing of the Suez Canal unless the contracts specified a route through the canal.

> Where there is an express provision in the contract
> covering the intervening event
> (ie a *force majeure* clause).

But a *force majeure* clause will be interpreted narrowly as in *Metropolitan Water Board v Dick Kerr & Co* (1918) where a reference to 'delays' was held to refer only to ordinary delays, and not to a delay caused by government decree.

A *force majeure* clause will not in any case be applied to cover trading with an enemy.

Where the frustration is self-induced.

A contract will not be frustrated if the event making performance impossible was the voluntary action of one of the parties. If the party concerned had a choice open to him, and chose to act in such a way as to make performance impossible, then the frustration will be self-induced and the court will refuse to treat the contract as discharged.

- In *The Superservant Two* (1990) one of two barges owned by the defendants and used to transport oil rigs was sunk. They were therefore unable to fulfill their contract to transport an oil-rig belonging to the plaintiff as their other barge (*Superservant One*) was already allocated to other contracts. The court held that the contract was not frustrated. The plaintiffs had another barge available, but chose not to allocate it to the contract with the plaintiffs.

This case illustrates both the courts reluctance to apply the doctrine of frustration and the advantage of using a *force majeure* clause.

Where the event was foreseeable.

If by reason of special knowledge, the event was foreseeable by one party, then he cannot claim frustration.

- In *Amalgamated Investment and Property Co v John Walker & Sons Ltd* (1976) the possibility that a building could be listed was foreseen by the plaintiff who had inquired about the matter beforehand. A failure to obtain planning permission was also foreseeable and was a normal risk for property developers. The contract was therefore not frustrated.

The effect of frustration

> At common law, the loss lay where it fell, ie the date of the frustrating event was all important. Anything paid or payable before that date would have to be paid. Anything payable after that date need not be paid.

This rule could be very unfair in its operation, as in *Chandler v Webster* (1904), where the hirer had to pay all the sum due despite the court holding the contract frustrated on account of the cancellation of the coronation.

> In the *Fibrosa* case (1943) the House of Lords did move away from this rule and held that where there was a total failure of consideration, then any money paid or payable in advance would have to be returned.

This rule, however, would only apply in the event of a total failure of consideration, and could itself in any case cause hardship if the other party had expended a considerable amount of money in connection with the contract.

> The Law Reform (Frustrated Contracts) Act 1943 was therefore passed to remedy these deficiencies. It provided:
>
> s 1(2) – all sums paid or payable before the frustrating event shall be recoverable or cease to be payable, but the court has a discretionary power to allow the payee to set off against the sum so paid expenses he has incurred before the frustrating event.
>
> s 1(3) – where one party has obtained a valuable benefit, before the time of discharge, the other party may recover from him such sums as the court considers just.

Note these two sections are to be applied independently. The expenses in s 1(2) can only be recovered from 'sums paid or payable before the frustrating event'.

Section 1(3) was applied in *BP Exploration v Hunt* (1982) where it was held that the court must:

- Identify and value the 'benefit obtained'.
- Assess the 'just sum' which it is proper to award.

The court also stated that:

- The section was designed to prevent unjust enrichment, not to apportion the loss, or to place the parties in the position they would be in had the contract been performed, or to restore them to their pre-contract position.

- In assessing the valuable benefit, the section required reference to the end benefit received by a party, not the cost of performance. In assessing the end benefit, the effect of the frustrating event had to be taken into account.

- The cost of performance can be taken into account in assessing the just sum.

In *BP v Hunt*, BP were to do the exploration and provide the necessary finance on an oil concession owned by Mr Hunt in Libya. They were also to provide certain 'farm-in' payments in cash and oil. In return, they were to get a half-share in the concession and 5% of their expenditure in reimbursement oil. A large field was discovered, the oil began to flow; then in 1971 the Libyan government nationalised the field.

The court held –

- The valuable benefit to Hunt was the net amount of oil received plus the compensation paid to the Libyan government which amounted to £85,000,000.

- The just sum would cover the work done by BP less the value of the reimbursement oil already received. This was assessed at £34,000,000. As the valuable benefit exceeded the just sum BP recovered their expenses in full. The position would have been very different, however, if the field had been nationalised at an earlier stage and no compensation had been paid.

The Law Reform (Frustrated Contracts) Act 1943 does not apply to

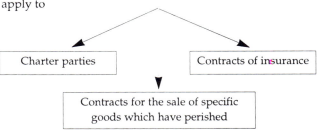

| Charter parties | Contracts of insurance |

Contracts for the sale of specific goods which have perished

9 Remedies for breach of contract and restitution

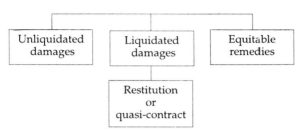

Unliquidated damages (ie damages assessed by the court)

The purpose of unliquidated damages is to compensate the plaintiff for the loss he has suffered as a result of a breach.

not

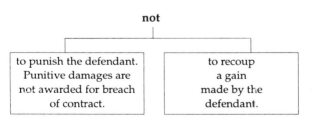

If no loss has been suffered, then nominal damages only will be awarded.

- In *Surrey CC v Bredero Homes* (1993) the court refused to award damages against a defendant who had not complied with planning permission as there was no loss to the council.

- However, in *Chaplin v Hicks* (1911) damages were awarded for the loss of a chance to win a competition, although there was no certainty that the plaintiff would have been one of the winners.

Methods of compensating the plaintiff

Expectation ie, loss of bargain the traditional basis for assessing damages in contract. It aims to put the plaintiff in the same position, as far as money can do it, as if the contract had been performed.	Reliance ie, out of pocket or wasted expenditure, the normal way for assessing damages in tort.

- But because 'expectation' damages would be difficult to assess, damages on a reliance basis were awarded for breach of contract in *McRae v Commonwealth Disposals Commission* (1951) to cover expenses incurred in searching for a wreck which did not exist.

  Also in *Anglia Television v Reed* (1972) where the leading actor repudiated his contract at the last moment, the plaintiffs were able to recover all their wasted expenditure on the programme, including even those incurred before the contract had been signed.

  But cf *Regalian Properties v London Dockland Development* (1995) where expenses incurred while negotiations were expressly 'subject to contract' were not recoverable.

- It has been held that a plaintiff may freely choose between expectation and reliance damages, unless he has made a 'bad bargain'. In *C&P Haulage v Middleton* (1983) the plaintiff hired a garage for six months on the basis that any improvements would become the property of the landlord. He was ejected in breach of contract, and sued for the cost of the improvements. Held – expenditure would have been wasted even if the contract had been performed.

  It is for the defendant to prove that the plaintiff had made a bad bargain as in *CCC Films v Impact Quadrant Films* (1985) where the defendant failed to prove that the plaintiff would not have made a profit from distributing the films had they been delivered in accordance with the contract.

- In normal circumstances, the plaintiff will ask for damages on an expectation basis, as this is more profitable for him.

Contributory negligence

This is only relevant where the liability in contract is identical with the liability on tort, ie the breach is of a contractual duty to take care (*Barclays Bank v Fairclough Building* (1994)).

Quantification of damage

Where 'loss of bargain' damages are claimed there are two possible methods of quantification.

| Difference in value | Cost of cure |

The court will normally adopt the most appropriate (*Ruxley Electronics and Construction v Forsyth* (1995)).

Prima facie rules

Sale of goods – difference in value.

Failure to repair (lease) – difference in value.

Building contracts – cost of cure.

eg contracts for the sale of goods.

Failure to deliver

The Sale of Goods Act 1979 states damages will represent the difference between the contract price and the market price.

- In *Williams Bros v Agius* (1914) the profit which would have been earned on a resale was ignored; damages represented the difference between the contract price and the market price.

Failure to accept delivery and pay

The Sale of Goods Act 1979 states that damages will again represent the difference between the contract price and the market price.

- But if the seller is a dealer in mass produced goods, then the damage to him will be the loss of profit on one transaction. The plaintiff had sold one item less than he otherwise would have during the year (*Thomson v Robinson* (1955)).

- However, if the mass produced item is in short supply and the number of sales is governed by supply not by demand, then there is no loss of profit and damages would not be awarded (*Charter v Sullivan* (1957)).

- The damages revert to the difference between the contract price and market price in the case of second hand goods even if the seller is a dealer (*Lazenby Garages v Wright* (1976)).

Limitations on principle of expectation

Although the stated aim of the expectation basis of assessing damages is to put the plaintiff in the position he would have been in had the contract been performed, there are a number of rules which militate against this result.

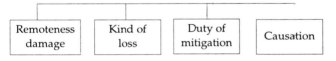

| Remoteness damage | Kind of loss | Duty of mitigation | Causation |

Remoteness of damage

> Damages cannot be recovered for losses that are too remote. The losses must be 'within the reasonable contemplation' of the parties.

- In *Hadley v Baxendale* (1854) a mill was closed because of the delay of a carrier in returning a mill shaft. The court held that the carrier was not liable for damages for the closure of the mill as he was not aware that the absence of a mill shaft would lead to this conclusion.

The following damages were said to be recoverable:

- ❍ Those arising naturally out of the breach.

- ❍ Those which because of special knowledge would have been within the contemplation of the parties.

- In *Victoria Laundry v Newman Industries* (1949) the rule was restated, and based on knowledge. The laundry was able to recover damages for normal loss of profit following a delay in the delivery of a boiler, but not for specially lucrative dyeing contracts they were offered during this time.

Damages were said to be recoverable for losses which were 'reasonably foreseeable' (a phrase also used in tort) either from:

- ❍ Imputed knowledge; or

- ❍ Actual knowledge.

- In *The Heron II* (1969) the House of Lords stated that a higher degree of forseeability is required in contract than in tort. Damages were awarded to cover losses arising from the late delivery of sugar to Basra. It was foreseeable that the price of sugar in Basra might fluctuate. For a loss to be foreseeable, there must be:

- ❍ 'a real danger';

- ❍ 'a serious possibility';

or the loss was

- ❍ 'not unlikely';

- ❍ 'liable to result'.

The difference between the tests of remoteness in contract and tort has been criticised, but justified on the ground that a contracting party can protect himself against unusual risks by drawing them to the attention of the other party to the contract.

Application of remoteness rules

- Imputed knowledge

  Hadley v Baxendale (1854)
  Victoria Laundry v Newman Industries (1949)
  The Heron II (1967)

- Actual knowledge

  Defendants knowledge of special circumstances must be precise. This encourages contracting parties to disclose clearly any exceptional losses in advance.

  In *Simpson v L&NWR* (1876) the defendant was liable for loss caused to the plaintiff by delivering goods to Newcastle Show Ground the day after the show had finished.

  In *Horne v Midland Railway* (1873) defendants were held not liable for exceptionally high profit lost by plaintiff through late delivery. They knew that shoes would have to be taken back if not delivered on 3 February, but not that the plaintiff would lose an exceptionally high profit.

> Note, the test of remoteness determines entitlement, not quantum.

- In *Wroth v Tyler* (1974) the defendant was liable for the full difference between the contract price and the market price, although the rise in the market price was exceptional and could not have been foreseen.

- In *Parsons (Livestock) Ltd v Uttley Ingham Co Ltd* (1978) the defendants who had supplied inadequately ventilated hoppers for pig food were held liable for the loss of the plaintiffs pigs, even though the disease from which they died was not foreseeable. It was enough that they could have contemplated any illness of the pigs. (But *cf Victoria Laundry v Newman Industries* (1849).)

Lord Denning in this case argued that so far as physical damage was concerned (not loss of profit), all direct losses should be recoverable, as in tort.

Lord Scarman has also stated that it would be ridiculous if the amount of damages depended on whether an action was framed in contract or tort. A House of Lords' decision is awaited.

It is sometimes disputed that the decisions since *Hadley v Baxendale* have not in any way clarified the rule.

Types of loss recognised

Pecuniary loss

This is the normal ground for the award of damages for breach of contract.

Non-pecuniary loss

However, damages for non-pecuniary loss will be awarded in specific cases eg

• Pain and suffering consequent on physical injury;

• Physical inconvenience

In *Watts v Morrow* (1991) damages were awarded to cover the inconvenience of living in a house whilst it was being repaired;

• Damage to commercial reputation.

In *Gibbons v Westminster Bank* (1939) damages were awarded to cover the losses caused by the wrongful referring of a cheque.

Cf Malik v BCCI (1995) where the Court of Appeal held that no compensation was payable for the stigma of having worked for an organisation which had been run corruptly.

- Distress to plaintiff

Traditionally damages for injured feelings were not awarded for breach of contract.

Addis v Gramaphone Co (1909)

However, in recent years exceptions were developed to this rule.

○ Damages for disappointment were awarded against a holiday company in *Jarvis v Swan Tours* (1973) where the holiday was not as described.

○ In *Hayes v Dodd* (1990) the Court of Appeal confirmed that damages for distress are not recoverable in normal commercial contracts, but could be recovered in contracts:

to provide pleasure. See *Jarvis v Swan Tours Ltd* (1973).	to prevent distress. *Heywood v Wellers* (1976) – solicitor's failure to obtain an injunction.

It has been suggested that damages for distress are particularly appropriate in 'consumer contracts' ('consumer surplus'?).

The duty of mitigation

> The plaintiff has a duty to take reasonable steps
> to mitigate his loss.

In *Payzu v Saunders* (1919) the plaintiff had refused the
offer of goods at below market price. In *Brace v Calder*
(1895) an employee dismissed by a partnership turned
down an offer of similar employment by one of the partners. In both cases, the plaintiff was penalised for his failure to mitigate.

- He need not, however, take 'unreasonable' steps in miti-
gation.

  In *Pilkington v Wood* (1953) it was stated that the plaintiff
  did not need to embark on hazardous legal action in mit-
  igation of his loss. He should not take unreasonable steps
  which would increase losses.

- The plaintiff cannot recover damages for losses he has
avoided.

  In *British Westinghouse v Underground Electric Railways Co*
  (1912) the plaintiff replaced a defective turbine with a
  new turbine which was so much more efficient that the
  savings exceeded the losses on the defective turbine. Held
  – no loss – no damages.

- Note the duty to mitigate does not arise until there has
been an actual breach of contract, or an anticipatory
breach has been accepted by the other party (see *White
and Carter v McGregor* (above)).

Causation (losses which the defendant did not cause)

> The breach must have caused the loss as well as having preceded the loss.

- The action of a third party may break the chain of causation if it is not foreseeable.

  In *Lambert v Lewis* (1981) a farmer continued to use a coupling even though he knew it was broken. Held – the farmer was responsible; the manufacturer could not have foreseen that he would continue to use it knowing it was faulty.

- However, where the action is foreseeable, the chain of causation will not be broken.

  In *Stansbie v Troman* (1948) a painter who, in breach of contract, had left a door unlocked, was held liable for goods taken by thieves, since this was the kind of loss he had undertaken to guard against by locking the doors.

Liquidated damages

Damages set by the parties themselves.

> The parties may stipulate that a certain sum must be paid on a breach of contract.

> If the sum represents a genuine pre-estimate, then it will be enforced by the court as liquidated damages.

> If the sum is not genuine, but is an attempt to frighten the other party into performing, then it is a penalty. A penalty will not be enforced by court.

The following guidelines for distinguishing between the two were suggested in *Dunlop Pneumatic Tyre Ltd v New Garage & Motor Co* (1915).

- A penalty – if the sum is extravagant and unconscionable.

- A penalty – if a larger sum is payable on the failure to pay a smaller sum.

- A penalty – if the same sum is payable on major and minor breaches.

- It is no obstacle to the sum being liquidated damages that a precise pre-estimate is almost impossible.

> Penalty clauses will not be enforced by the court. Instead the court will award unliquidated damages.

The rule against penalties does not apply to:

- Acceleration clauses

  Here, the whole of a debt becomes payable immediately if certain conditions are not observed.

- Deposits

  Money paid otherwise than on a breach of contract

  Alder v Moore (1961)

  Bridge v Campbell Discount Co Ltd (1962)

- clauses declaring a term a condition

  London North Central v Butterworth

Equitable remedies

Specific performance

> An order of the court directing the defendant to
> fulfill his obligations under the contract.

Traditionally, specific performance will only be awarded
where damages are not an adequate remedy, ie

> Where the plaintiff cannot get a satisfactory
> substitute, eg contracts for the sale of land, or
> contracts for the sale of goods which cannot be
> obtained elsewhere eg, antiques, valuable paintings
> – unless bought as an investment,
> as in *Cohen v Roche* (1927).

> Where damages are difficult to assess eg, annuities.

> Where there is no alternative remedy available
> (*Beswick v Beswick* (1968)) see above.

All equitable remedies are discretionary

The following will be taken into account.

- Mutuality – negative – a minor cannot get it because it is
  not available against a minor. Positive – a vendor of land
  may obtain it although damages would be an adequate
  remedy, because it is available to a purchaser of land.

- Supervision. The need for constant supervision prevented the appointment of a resident porter being ordered in *Ryan v Mutual Tontine Association* (1893) but in *Posner v Scott Lewis* (1986) a similar order was made because the terms of the contract were sufficiently precise.

- Impossibility – *Watts v Spence* (1976) – land belonged to a third party.

- Hardship – *Patel v Ali* (1984) – defendant would lose the help of supportive neighbours.

- Conduct of the plaintiff – *Shell (UK) Ltd v Lostock Garages* (1977) – Shell's behaviour was unreasonable.

- Vagueness – *Tito v Waddell* (1977) see above.

- Mistake – *Webster v Cecil* (1861) – see above.

Special problems

- Contracts of personal service.

  These are considered to involve personal relationships and are therefore not thought suitable for an order of specific performance.

  However, in two recent cases, such orders were made – *Hill v CA Parsons Ltd* (1972) and *Irani v Southampton AHA* (1985) on the ground that in the very unusual circumstances of those cases, the mutual trust between the employer and employee had not been destroyed.

Building contracts

  The courts are reluctant to enforce building contracts on the grounds that damages are generally an adequate remedy; the terms are often vague; there are difficulties with supervision.

But it was held in *Wolverhampton Corpn v Emmons* (1901) that provided the terms were clear the problem of supervision would not be an absolute barrier.

Injunctions

> These are orders directing the defendant
> not to do a certain act.

Types of injunction

Prohibitory injunction

This is an order commanding the defendant not to do something.

Mandatory injunction

This orders the defendant to undo something he had agreed not to.

Interlocutory injunction

This is designed to regulate the position of the parties pending trial.

Injunctions are also discretionary remedies and are subject to the similar constraints to orders of specific performance. However, an injunction will be granted to enforce a negative stipulation in a contract of employment, as long as this is not an indirect way of enforcing the contract.

- *Warner Bros v Nelson* (1937);

- *cf Page One Records v Britton* (1968).

A comparison of the remedies for misrepresentation and for breach of contract

Setting aside contracts

	Termination or rescission for breach
Breach	Available only for breaches of conditions, fundamental breaches of innominate terms and repudiations.
	Contract discharged from time of breach; discharge not retrospective. Innocent party can also sue for damages (see Chapter 8).
	Rescission
Misrepresentation	Available for all misrepresentations, but at discretion of court, and subject to certain bars. Contract cancelled prospectively and retrospectively; parties returned to the position they were in before the contract was entered into (see Chapter 6).

Damages	
Breach	Damages available as of right. Normally assessed on expectation basis. Losses must be within the contemplation of the parties. See above.
	Damages available in tort of deceit; negligent statements; and under s 2(1) Misrepresentation Act 1967.
Misrepresentation	Damages assessed on reliance basis. All losses flowing directly from misrepresentation will be covered, whether or not foreseeable, in actions in deceit, and under s 2(1) Misrepresentation Act (*Royscot v Rogerson* (1991)). Losses must be foreseeable in the tort of negligence. No right to damages for innocent misrepresentation but may be awarded in lieu of rescission at the discretion of the court.

Exclusion clauses	
Breach	see ss 3, 6, 7 UCTA.
Misrepresentation	all clauses must be reasonable.

Restitution or quasi-contract (based on unjust enrichment)

Restitution may be available where parties are not in a contractual relationship.

It is based on the principle of unjust enrichment; it allows the injured party to recover money paid or the value of benefits conferred, where it would be unjust to allow the other party to retain the benefit.

It covers:

recovery of money   payment for work done

Money may be recovered

• Where there is a total failure of consideration (see *Fibrosa* case (frustration)).

In *Rowland v Divall* (1923) the plaintiff had bought a car which turned out to be stolen property, and which was recovered by the owner. Despite the fact that the plaintiff had had the use of the car for a considerable time, and it had fallen in value during this time, the plaintiff was able to recover the full purchase price of the car from the defendant. There had been a total failure of consideration.

- Money paid under a mistake of fact, is recoverable, provided the mistake is as to a fact which, if true, would have legally or morally obliged the plaintiff to pay the money, or is sufficiently serious to require payment, eg

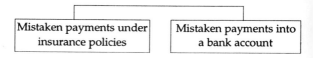

| Mistaken payments under insurance policies | Mistaken payments into a bank account |

- Money made under a void contract

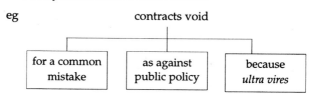

eg   contracts void

| for a common mistake | as against public policy | because *ultra vires* |

- In *Westdeutche Landesbank v Islington LBC* (1994) the council had entered into a rate swapping arrangement with the bank, under which the bank had paid £2,500,000 to the council in advance. The council had paid approximately £1,200,00 to the bank by instalment, and argued that since there was not a total failure of consideration, it should not have to pay the bank the remaining £1,300,000. The Court of Appeal held that the principle upon which money must be repaid under a void contract is different from that on a total failure of consideration. Recovery of money under a void contract is allowed if there is no legal basis for such a payment.

- Note money paid under contract which is void for illegality cannot be recovered, unless the action can be framed without relying on the contract.

Parkinson v Royal College of Ambulance (1925)

Bowmakers v Barnet Instruments (1945)

Tinsley v Milligan (1993)

- Note, recovery under these heads will not be possible if:

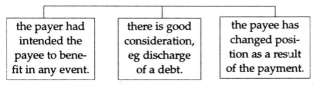

| the payer had intended the payee to benefit in any event. | there is good consideration, eg discharge of a debt. | the payee has changed position as a result of the payment. |

In *Lipkin Gorman v Karpnale Ltd* (1992) a partner in a firm of solicitors was a compulsive gambler who regularly gambled at a casino run by the defendants. In order to finance his gambling, he had drawn cheques on client accounts where he was the sole signatory. He had spent at least £154,000 of this money at the defendant's casino, and the plaintiff sued for the return of the money, as money had been received under contract which was void (declared void by statute). Held – where the true owner of stolen money sought to recover it from an innocent third party, the recipient was under an obligation to return it where he had given no consideration for it, unless he could show that he had altered his position in good faith. In this case, the plaintiff was able to recover the £154,000 less the winnings paid to the partner. The casino had altered their position on each gamble in that they had become vulnerable to a loss.

However, in *South Tyneside Metropolitan Borough Council v Svenska International* (1994) the House of Lords allowed the council to recover approximately £200,000 it had paid to a bank under a rate swap agreement which had been declared *ultra vires* and void. The court rejected the bank's claim that it had changed its position in that it had entered into financial arrangements with other organisations in order to hedge its losses.

- Money paid to a third party for the benefit of the defendant provided the plaintiff was not acting as a volunteer (eg a mother paying off a sons debt), but was acting under some constraint.

In *Macclesfield Corpn v Great Central Railway* (1911) the plaintiffs carried out repairs to a bridge which the defendants were legally obliged (but had refused) to maintain. They were regarded as purely volunteers, and could not therefore recover the money. However, in *Exall v Partridge* (1799) the plaintiff paid off arrears of rent owed by the defendant in order to avoid seizure of the plaintiff's carriage which was kept on the defendant's premises. The plaintiff was acting under a constraint, and could therefore recover the money.

Payment for work done

> Here, the plaintiff is seeking compensation on a *quantum meruit* basis (*cf* s 1(3) Frustrated Contracts Act).

- Where the plaintiff has prevented performance of the contract (see *Planché v Colburn* (1831)).
- Where work has been carried out under a void contract. In *Craven Ellis v Canons Ltd* (1936) the plaintiff had carried out a great deal of work on behalf of a company on the understanding that he had been appointed managing director. It was later discovered that he had not properly been appointed managing director. The court held that he should be paid on a *quantum meruit* basis for the work he had done.

- Where agreement has not been reached, and

  ○ The work was requested by the defendants. In *William Lacey v Davis* (1957) the plaintiffs had submitted the lowest tender for a building contract, and had been led to believe that they would be awarded it. At the defendants' request, they then prepared various plans and estimates. The defendants then decided not to proceed. The court ordered the defendants to pay a reasonable sum on a *quantum meruit* basis for the work that had been done, on analogy with *Craven Ellis v Cannons*; or

  ○ The work had been freely accepted. In *British Steel Corpn v Cleveland Bridge Engineering Co* (1984) a letter of intent was issued by the defendants, indicating that they intended to enter into a contract with the plaintiffs for the construction and delivery of cast-steel 'nodes'. However, it proved impossible to reach agreement on a number of major items. Despite this, a number of 'nodes' were eventually constructed, and accepted by the defendants. It was held by the court that the defendants should pay for the nodes they had accepted.

10 Privity of contract

Only a party to a contract can sue on a contract.	Only a party to a contract can be sued on a contract.

In *Tweddle v Atkinson* (1861) the plaintiff had married Mr Guy's daughter. The plaintiff's father and Mr Guy, had agreed together that that they would each pay a sum of money to the plaintiff. Mr Guy died before the money was paid, and the plaintiff sued his executors. The action was dismissed – the plaintiff was not a party to to the contract, which was made between the two fathers. See also *Beswick v Beswick*.

In *Dunlop v Selfridges* (1915) Dew & Co, at the instigation of Dunlop, had placed a minimum resale price in their contract with Selfridges.

Held – Dunlop could not sue Selfridges for breach of contract; they were not parties to the contract, nor had they given consideration to Selfridges.

Privity of contract is closely associated with the rule that consideration must move from the promisee. See *Dunlop v Selfridges* (above).

Matters relevant to the doctrine of privity

Matters traditionally outside the doctrine of privity.	Attempts to confer benefits on third parties.	Attempts to impose obligations on third parties.

Matters traditionally outside the doctrine

It has been argued that it is only because English law has declared many transactions not to be subject to the doctrine of privity that the doctrine itself has survived so long.

Assignment	Agency
Rights can be assigned provided that certain formalities are followed.	A principal can sue and be sued on contracts made by an agent on his behalf.

Trusts	Multipartite agreements
Where a trust has been created, the beneficiary under the trust can sue the trustees even if he was not a party to the original agreement.	In *Clarke v Dunraven* (1897) entrants in a yacht race were allowed to sue each other. The Companies Act allows shareholders to sue each other.

Collateral contracts

In limited cases, the court will find a separate (collateral) contract between the promisor and the third party
(*Shanklin Pier v Detel Products* (1951)).

Land law recognises a number of exceptions.

Leases

The benefits and obligations under a lease can be transferred to third parties.

Law of Property Act 1925, s 56

See below.

Restrictive covenants

These can bind a third party under the rule in *Tulk v Moxhay* (1848).

Statutory exceptions

- Price maintenance agreements.
- Various insurance contracts.
- eg Married Woman's Property Act.
- Law of Property Act 1925, s 56
- Negotiable instruments.

Attempts to confer benefits on a third party

```
                    ┌──────────────┴──────────────┐
┌────────────────────────────┐   ┌────────────────────────────┐
│   Allowing the third       │   │  Allowing the promisee     │
│   party to sue.            │   │  to sue on behalf of the   │
│                            │   │  third party.              │
└────────────────────────────┘   └────────────────────────────┘
```

Attempts to allow the third party to sue

- Attempts to extend the use of 'trusts'.

  ○ In *Walford's* case (1919) under a charter party, the shipowner promised the charterer to pay a broker a commission. Held – the charterer was trustee of this promise for the broker, who could thus enforce it against the shipowner.

  ○ However in *Re Schebsman* (1944) a contract between Schebsman and X Ltd, that in certain circumstances his wife and daughter should be paid a lump sum, was held not to create a trust.

  The trust as a device to outflank privity was limited by the courts, presumably because of concern that the irrevocable nature of the trust may prevent the contracting parties from changing their minds and the courts no longer go out of their way to find that the parties intended to create a trust.

- Lord Denning launched a campaign against privity, and argued that s 56 intended to destroy doctrine altogether. This was finally rejected by the House of Lords in *Beswick v Beswick* (1968); they acknowledged that the wording (see above) was wide enough to support Lord Denning's view, but insisted, nevertheless, that it must be restricted to the law of real property as the purpose of the Act was to consolidate the law relating to real property.

- Agency

Agency has been used to allow a third party to take advantage of an exclusion clause in a contract to which he was not a party.

○ The House of Lords refused to allow stevedores to rely on an exclusion clause in a contract between the carriers and the cargo owner in *Scruttons v Midland Silicones* (1962) on the basis that only a party to the contract could claim the benefit of the contract, ie the exclusion clause.

○ However, in *The Eurymedon* (1975) the Privy Council, on similar facts, held that the carriers had negotiated a second contract (a collateral contract) as agents of the stevedores, and the stevedores could claim the benefit of the exclusion clause in this contract.

○ But in *Southern Water Authority v Carey* (1985) sub-contractors sought to rely on a limitation of liability clause in a main contract. Held – they must have specific authority to negotiate on behalf of a third party, before this device could work.

○ In *Norwich City Council v Harvey* (1989) instead of using an exclusion clause, the contract placed the risk of loss or damage by fire on the owner, and this protected both main contractor and sub-contractor.

Attempts to allow the promisee to enforce the contract on behalf of the third party
- Specific performance

In *Beswick v Beswick* (1968) Peter Beswick had transferred his business to his nephew, in return for his nephew's promise to pay his uncle a pension, and after his death, an annuity to his widow. The nephew paid his uncle the pension, but only one payment of the annuity was made. The widow as administratrix of her husband's estate, successfully sued her nephew for specific performance of the contract to pay the annuity, although the House of Lords implied that she would not have succeeded if she had been suing in her own right.

- Injunction

Similarly, an injunction may be awarded to restrain a breach of a negative promise on a suit brought by the promisee, eg A promised B not to compete with C, or by a stay of proceedings.

In *Snelling v Snelling Ltd* (1973) three brothers lent money to a family company, and agreed not to reclaim the money for a certain period. A stay of proceedings was granted to one of the brothers to stop another brother from breaking his promise and suing the company for the return of his money.

- Damages

Damages to cover the disappointment of a third party was sanctioned by Lord Denning in *Jackson v Horizon Holidays Ltd* (1975) where the plaintiff entered into a contract with a holiday firm for a holiday for his family and himself in Ceylon. The holiday was a disaster. The plaintiff recovered damages for £500 for 'mental stress'. On appeal, the court confirmed the amount, on the ground that witnessing the distress of his family had increased the plaintiff's own distress. Lord Denning, however, stated that the sum was excessive for the plaintiff's own distress, but upheld the award on the ground that the plaintiff had made the contract on behalf of himself and of his wife and children, and that he could recover in respect of their loss as well as their own.

This statement by Lord Denning was disapproved by the House of Lords in *Woodar Investment Development Ltd v Wimpey Construction (UK) Ltd* (1980) where the plaintiffs agreed to sell land to the defendants for £850,000. It was also agreed that the defendants should pay part of this amount (£1,500) to a third party. The plaintiffs sued for damages for breach of contract, and asked for damages for the loss to the third party. The House of Lords held that there was no repudiatory breach of contract but went on to discuss the privity issue, and disapproved of Lord Dennings statement in *Jackson v Horizon Holidays*. They stated that damages should not be recovered on behalf of a third party.

Lord Wilberforce, however, did suggest that there was a special category of contracts which called for special treatment where one party contracted for a benefit to be shared equally between a group, eg family holidays, ordering meals in restaurants for a party, hiring taxis for a group and that the decision in *Jackson* could be supported on this ground (this could be done on the basis of agency as in *Lockett v Charles* (1938) where it was held that the wife was the contracting party with the hotel, although the husband ordered and paid for the meal).

There is as yet, however, no appellate court decision where this suggestion has been applied.

Attempts to impose obligations on third parties

- Restrictive covenants inserted into a contract for the sale of land may bind subsequent purchasers, provided:

  - they are negative in nature;

  - the subsequent purchaser has notice of the covenants;

○ the person claiming the benefit has land capable of benefiting from its enforcement (*Tulk v Moxhay* (1848));

- The court extended the rule in *Tulk v Moxhay* to personal property, eg a ship in *The Strathcona* (1926) where the plaintiffs had chartered *The Strathcona* for certain months each year. The ship was sold to the defendant who refused to allow the plaintiff to use the ship. The plaintiff sought an injunction on the ground that the doctrine in *Tulk v Moxhay* should be extended from land to ships. The court granted an injunction.

This decision was criticised in *Port Line Ltd v Ben Line Ltd* (1958) where a ship chartered to the plaintiff was sold to the defendants. The ship was requisitioned during the Suez war, and compensation was paid to the defendants. This compensation was claimed by the plaintiffs. Held – even if *The Strathcona* case was rightly decided, it could not be applied in this case as (a) the defendant was not in breach of any duty and (b) the plaintiff had not sought an injunction but financial compensation which was outside *Tulk v Moxhay*.

The decision in *The Strathcona* has been widely criticised because:

○ contract of hire creates personal, not proprietary rights in the hired object;

○ the retention of land which can benefit from the covenant is a necessary condition of the doctrine in *Tulk v Moxhay*.

- However, in *Swiss Bank Corpn v Lloyds Bank* (1979) Browne-Wilkinson J considered that the decision in *The Strathcona* was correct. He suggested, however, that the tort of inducing a breach of contract or knowingly interfering with a contract would be a more suitable basis for the decision than *Tulk v Moxhay*, and stated that in his judgment a person proposing to deal with property in such a way as to cause a breach of a contract affecting that property will be restrained by injunction from doing so if when he acquired that property he had actual knowledge of the contract.

Criticism of the doctrine of privity

> The doctrine has been much criticised, particularly the rule which prevents a third party from enforcing a contract.

Suggested reasons for the doctrine:

- principle of mutuality; only a party who can be sued on a contract should be able to sue on it;

- the freedom of parties to vary an agreement would be restricted if third party rights were created;

- third party beneficiaries are often gratuitous, and allowing them to sue would interfere with the doctrine of consideration.

Criticisms

- It is said to destroy the legitimate expectations of third parties.

- It is not found in the law of Scotland or the USA.

- Lord Denning has alleged that it is a 19th century innovation, and has even doubted its existence. He attacked the doctrine in *Scruttons v Midland Silicones* (above), *Beswick v Beswick* (above) and *Jackson v Horizon Holidays* (above). But the doctrine was confirmed by the House of

Lords in *Beswick v Beswick* and in *Woodar Investment Development Ltd v Wimpey*.

- However, in *Beswick* Lord Reid stated that if Parliament procrastinated further, 'this House might find it necessary to deal with the matter'.

- In *Woodar*, Lord Scarman hoped that if Parliament did not act, that 'this House will reconsider *Tweddle v Atkinson* and other cases which stand guard over this unjust rule'.

- In 1994, the Privy Council questioned whether English law should continue to maintain a strict rule of privity of contract.

In 1991 the Law Commission issued a consultation paper which recommended:

- that third parties should be allowed to enforce agreements made for their benefit, provided the contract indicated an intention to confer an enforceable legal obligation;

- the third party who sued under this provision would be subjected to any defences available to the promisor against the other contracting party;

- the commission also invited comments as to whether acceptance, adoption, or material reliance should be required before the parties are prevented from altering their agreement in a way which affects the third party.